PRAISE FOR *POLYSECURE*

"Anyone even considering nonmonogamy would benefit from reading *Polysecure*. Jessica Fern does an excellent job of not only explaining attachment theory and applying it to nonmonogamy but also offering real steps readers can take and skills they can hone to help create the secure, satisfying relationships they want."
—JoEllen Notte, sex educator and author of *The Monster Under the Bed: Sex, Depression, and the Conversations We Aren't Having*

"This is required reading for people in open relationships and should be used as a textbook for every therapist who works with people in polyamorous relationships."
—Kathy Labriola, counselor, nurse and author of *The Polyamory Breakup Book, The Jealousy Workbook* and *Love in Abundance*

"*Polysecure* gives people a way to understand how they may be recreating old patterns by bringing their own childhood attachment styles into their adult relationships. And even more importantly, it offers concrete skills for how to use this knowledge to create healthier, more satisfying and secure relationship dynamics."
—Max Rivers, intimacy coach and author of *Loving Conflict: How Conflict Is Really Your Relationship Trying to Go Deeper*

polysecure

polysecure

Attachment, Trauma and Consensual Nonmonogamy

Jessica Fern

with a foreword by Eve Rickert
and Nora Samaran

Polysecure

Attachment, Trauma and Consensual Nonmonogamy

Thornapple Press
300 – 722 Cormorant Street
Victoria, BC V8W 1P8 Canada
press@thornapplepress.ca

Thornapple Press is a brand of Talk Science to Me Communications Inc. and the successor to Thorntree Press. Our business offices are located in the traditional, ancestral and unceded territories of the ləkʷəŋən and W̱SÁNEĆ peoples.

Cover design by Brianna Harden
Interior design by Jeff Werner
Substantive editing by Andrea Zanin
Copy-editing by Hazel Boydell
Proofreading by Heather van der Hoop

Library of Congress Cataloging-in-Publication Data
    Names: Fern, Jessica, author.
    Title: Polysecure : attachment, trauma and consensual
        nonmonogamy / by Jessica Fern.
    Description: [Portland] : [Thorntree Press], [2020] |
        Includes bibliographical references and index.
    Identifiers: LCCN 2020009992 (print) | LCCN 2020009993 (ebook) |
        ISBN 9781944934989 (paperback) | ISBN 9781952125003 (kindle
        edition) | ISBN 9781944934996 (epub) | ISBN 9781952125010 (pdf)
    Subjects: LCSH: Nonmonogamous relationships--
        Psychological aspects. | Attachment behavior.
    Classification: LCC HQ980 .F47 2020 (print) | LCC HQ980 (ebook) |
        DDC 306.84/23--dc23
    LC record available at https://lccn.loc.gov/2020009992
    LC ebook record available at https://lccn.loc.gov/2020009993

10 9 8

Printed in Canada on sustainably sourced paper.

In loving dedication to Chris Kaminskas (1961–2009)
and my madrina, Maria Pusz (1947–2014).

You were the safe havens and secure
bases that I owe my resiliency to.

CONTENTS

FOREWORD

Eve

The literature on polyamory has come a long way since *The Ethical Slut* and *Polyamory: The New Love Without Limits* were first published in 1997. Both books broke new ground and offered a new identity and community for nonmonogamous people who had previously struggled in isolation. But these books were written from the perspectives of specific subcultures, and they didn't (couldn't!) deal with the full range of issues confronted by the newly polyamorous.

Options began to proliferate in the late 2000s, with books like *Opening Up* and many lesser-known titles. These offered a wider range of practical advice, but as the title *Opening Up* suggests, this wave of poly practice presumed the centrality of a primary couple and popularized a hierarchical model in which primary partners were to have rights and safety that secondary or casual partners were not granted to the same degree. Early polyamorous media representation through shows like *Polyamorous: Married and Dating* fiercely reinforced this view.

This was the kind of polyamory I was introduced to when I first began exploring in the early 2000s. The hierarchical relationship structures that were the norm in the online circles I frequented (and nearly all media representation of polyamory) kept some of the feeling of security offered by monogamy by protecting attachment needs, and often masking potential attachment disruptions, for those who were in so-called primary relationships. At the same time, they did a dismal job of honouring the attachment needs of partners who were considered "secondary": those outside a primary, usually presumed to be nesting, couple, whose bond was presumed to be more valid or worthy of protection than the others "opened up" to.

But some people were making noise. In 2003 the publication of "A Proposed Secondary's Bill of Rights" caused a stir in online polyamorous circles, and provided secondary partners with an important tool to advocate for their needs. Andie Nordgren published "The Short Instructional Manifesto for Relationship Anarchy" in 2006, questioning the need for relational hierarchies, and by the early 2010s, an increasing number of popular bloggers—many building on Nordgren's work—were pushing for recognition of a wider range of relationship styles, and in particular, of the needs of secondary partners.

Then, in 2014, my co-author and I published *More Than Two*, attempting to distill the last decade's worth of debate into an instructional manual that promised a non-hierarchical, more egalitarian way of thinking about polyamorous relationships.

When *More Than Two* encouraged polyamorous people to sweep away the external supporting structures of both monogamy and polyamorous hierarchy, though, what it offered in exchange fell short. It placed the onus of building security almost entirely on the individual who felt insecure. Despite the many people who were helped by the book, this inappropriate focus caused harm, and over time, I grew to understand there was something missing in our framework—I just didn't have the words for what.

It was Nora's blog, where in 2016 she proposed that "The Opposite of Rape Culture Is Nurturance Culture," that began to help me find words for what had been missing from *More Than Two*. I reached out to her on Twitter to talk about our work.

Naava

When Eve first said hello in summer 2016, we were both living in East Vancouver. My essay "The Opposite of Rape Culture Is Nurturance Culture" had gone viral earlier that year, and Eve reached out to talk shop.

Meeting over iced drinks at a little East Van cafe, we tossed around the idea of a collaboration combining attachment theory and ethical polyamory. We also quickly realized that we were neighbours who lived across the street from one another.

Over the next months we did what neighbours do: she invited me over to pick figs at her house and I dropped off some of the fig jam; we went for the occasional walk debating ethics and politics; I sometimes fed the cat. Life went on, as it does, and the idea moved to the back burner, as they do.

It was three years later when Eve sent me a link to a talk by Jessica Fern with a note: "Fern is doing what we talked about." I watched, fascinated, as Fern firmly drew connections between attachment theory and ethical polyamory with grace, style and wit.

Fern's intervention is a groundbreaking development in the trajectory of writing about ethical polyamory and relationships. The tools provided here will be helpful for those who are practising ethical polyamory; they will also help those who are monogamous, who also navigate dating, communicating needs, and making decisions about commitment. *Polysecure* expands on the existing literature in a significant—perhaps even paradigm-shifting—way.

Fern is uniquely qualified to write this book. She is a psychotherapist who is nonmonogamous and works with nonmonogamous people and families. She holds a master's in conflict analysis and resolution. Her insights come out of both professional training and extensive hands-on experience working with clients as a therapist. She has also experienced trauma, along with the nonlinear healing journey that follows.

In a sense, Fern's book picks up where *More Than Two* left off. Dubbed by many of its readers a sort of poly bible, *More Than Two* is one of the most popular and widely read polyamory guidebooks, and it remains relevant and useful today. Published by Thorntree Press in 2014, *More Than Two* moved the conversation along and changed the way many people think about and organize their relationships. But as Eve has reflected elsewhere, with all of its strengths, *More Than Two* also has drawbacks, as any book will.

As I've come to expect of Eve, when confronted with new insights and information she is willing, even eager, to look back over her own work and grow in ethics and analysis. This commitment to try, assess, seek out new insight and challenge, and change one's thinking is a professional practice I greatly respect. As publisher at Thorntree Press, Eve has helped bring this book out into the public conversation, and it promises to be pathbreaking.

In *Polysecure*, Jessica Fern has again moved the conversation forward. Although we cannot know for certain how a book will translate when it encounters the cultural context that receives it, my sense is that this book will increase the availability of tools for navigating needs, desires and commitments for those who want secure bonds; it will also offer vocabulary to aid in transparency for those who do not.

When done well, these conversations may help readers enjoy the possibilities—and fulfill the responsibilities—of fully informed consent.

As Fern so beautifully illustrates in these pages, true security builds in an interwoven way. It can be cultivated within, yes, but it grows in and through the bonds we share with others: in relationships, in communities and in the larger cultural fabric to which we belong.

The collaboration we discussed that summer day over coffee is no longer needed. This book has stepped into the gap and filled it, with rigour and care. I hope that readers will find it as calming, and as compelling, as I did when I first read the manuscript.

Eve Rickert, Victoria, BC
Naava Smolash, Vancouver, BC
July 2020

Eve Rickert is the co-author of *More Than Two: A Practical Guide to Ethical Polyamory* (Thorntree Press, 2014).
Naava Smolash, who sometimes writes under the pen name Nora Samaran, is the author of *Turn This World Inside Out: The Emergence of Nurturance Culture* (AK Press, 2019).

ACKNOWLEDGMENTS

Mom and Dad: Thank you for the spark of love that brought me into this world. Each of us has been through a shit ton in our lives and, as Mom would frequently say, *we did most of our growing up together*. Mom, thank you for your enthusiasm and unshakable support for whatever I do, as well as how much freedom you gave me to be me. Dad, thank you for your bravery and willingness to dive into some of the most difficult conversations a parent and child can have.

John Leporati: There would be no me without you and there would definitely be no writing without you. From my college entrance essay to job cover letters, to probably every significant paper I wrote in college and grad school, to this very book, you have been there for me like no other! Our bond has been unbreakable from day one and thank you for adopting me as yours.

Dave: Oh the irony that the first book I publish is the one piece of work that you weren't my ghostwriter for. Thank you for all of the ways that you have supported my writing through the years. You have such an incredible gift with language that I can only hope has rubbed off on me. Our marriage was also the testing ground for many of the personal insights that are captured in this book. Our ability to fluidly, lovingly and consciously navigate togetherness, separateness, connection and parenting is an *impossibly* precious gift. You will always be one of the most important attachments of my life.

Diego: Before you were born I knew how important it was for you to experience me as your safe haven and secure base, but I had no clue how profound my own healing of attachment would be through being your mother. Thank you for the fullness of your love.

Shane: Thank you for being the secure attachment love salve that my heart so desperately needed during our first year together. You stayed strong, secure and so sweet with me during my fearful flare-ups. You held me in the ways I needed, and when this book opportunity arose, you also challenged me to not lose sight of myself, my work-life balance or us while taking on this project. Thank you for keeping me in check. I'm so grateful for where we've already been and continually excited about where we're headed.

Eve Rickert, thank you immensely for this opportunity to create this book. Andrea Zanin, thank you for your valuable feedback regarding content, style and voice. Hazel Boydell, thank you for your support with copy-editing and tending to all the details. Heather van der Hoop, thank you for your detailed proofreading. Kate and Sarah, thank you for creating the space at Southwest Love Fest for Eve and me to connect. Nolan Lawless, thank you for geeking out with me about attachment and nonmonogamy. Our conversations and your insights have been important additions to my work.

To my ladies, Christy, Alexandra, Erin and Jessica. You have been my cheerleading team from the beginning of this process, both personally and professionally. Thank you for all of your encouragement and unwavering wholehearted support. Each of you means the world to me.

Finally, thank you to all of my clients. Our work together has been an enormous learning experience for me and I hope the insights that I've gained through our conversations will support everyone reading this book.

GLOSSARY

Compersion
The state of happiness, joy or pleasure that comes from delighting in other people's happiness. In nonmonogamy, this term is more specifically used to refer to the positive feelings experienced when your lover is having a positive experience with one of their other lovers.

Consensual nonmonogamy (CNM)
The practice of having multiple sexual and/or romantic partners at the same time, where all people involved are aware of this relationship arrangement and consent to it. CNM can include, but is not limited to, polyamory, swinging, open marriage, open relationship, solo polyamory and relationship anarchy.

Metamour
Two people who share a partner, but are not romantically or sexually involved with each other. For example, if you have a partner who also has a spouse, you and their spouse would be metamours, or if you have a boyfriend and a girlfriend who are not involved with each other, the two of them would be metamours to each other.

Monogamy
The practice of having one sexual or romantic partner at a time.

Mononormativity
This term was coined by Pieper and Bauer[1] to refer to the societal dominant assumptions regarding the naturalness and normalcy of monogamy, where political, popular and psychological narratives typically present monogamy as the superior, most natural or morally correct way to do relationships.

Polysaturated
The point at which the thought of another relationship leaves one feeling more exhausted than excited. When a polyamorous person has as many significant and insignificant others as they think they can handle at a given time.

INTRODUCTION

I'M WRITING THIS BOOK because I believe in love. Again and again, I have experienced the power of love to heal, to bridge, to connect and to awaken, as well as the trauma that ensues in its absence. In many ways my life is centered in not just believing in love, but in *being* love. That is, emanating love as best as I can, moment by moment, interaction by interaction. I am confident that many of you reading this also believe in love and that it is the desire to strengthen and deepen your love relationships that has led you to pick up this book.

My journey to writing this book officially began within the last year, but it really began 40 years ago, with my first attachment experiences as an infant and the multiple attachment ruptures that followed. A third-generation New Yorker, I grew up in the housing projects of Brooklyn in a neighborhood well-acquainted with violence and a family considerably impacted by multiple divorces, multi-generational traumas, sexual abuse, substance abuse, mental illness and interpersonal discord. These experiences had an impact that was challenging for many years, affecting all areas of my life, but they also created a powerful determination in me to not only thrive and be resilient in the face of my early childhood hardships but to also contribute to the healing and transformation of others who have been impacted by neglect, abuse, trauma and poverty. In wanting to understand how to heal the mind, body and heart, I began to study everything I could, from the spiritual to the academic. I devoted my life to the investigation of how we change, evolve and develop, how we can communicate healthily and effectively, how we can heal and become safely embodied in the wake of trauma, how we can unshackle our hearts from our survival-based reactivity and defenses, and how we can liberate our minds from bigotry, ignorance and internalized oppression.

As you can probably imagine, this led me to have a diverse professional life that crossed over several seemingly disparate intersections—I was both a socially engaged Buddhist and a somatic bodyworker, a genocide researcher and a therapist. About a decade into my healing practice with individuals, I began to expand my psychotherapy practice to include couples work. In the earlier stages of building up my client base of couples, there was one particular week in which three different couples' sessions included one of the partners bringing up their desire to explore polyamory for the first time. Needless to say, this caught my attention. I knew about polyamory from a personal perspective, but professionally I was at a loss. Nonmonogamy was barely mentioned in any of my training and when it was mentioned, it was usually dismissed or disparaged. One of the couples I was working with mentioned that they were reading the book *Sex at Dawn: The Prehistoric Origins of Modern Sexuality,* in which authors Christopher Ryan and Cacilda Jethá discuss the evolution of monogamy as being relatively recent in human history. So, like any decent (and underinformed) therapist I quickly bought the book to better support them in our work together. To my surprise, reading *Sex at Dawn* turned out to be a personal awakening. Within the pages of the book I found descriptions of myself I didn't know existed and desires that had lain dormant for years. As a bisexual woman, I was often confused about how to reconcile my sexuality within a monogamous relationship with either a man or a woman. Even though I already knew a decent amount about polyamory, it was mainly from a second- or third-person perspective where polyamory was something *you* or *they* did. It wasn't until reading *Sex at Dawn* that I finally identified with polyamory from a first-person perspective, realizing that not only had I already practiced forms of nonmonogamy for years in my late adolescence and early twenties, but that it was also what I felt to be the fullest expression of my love and sexuality now.

This all happened while I was in a monogamous marriage, so immediately throwing off the relational restraints of monogamy to more fully express my capacity and desire to love more than one person was not something that I could just do the very next day. But the personal realizations that came from reading the book impacted not only myself, but also my marriage and my family. Thankfully, after many long walks and talks with my then-husband, he was willing to take on the transition from monogamy to polyamory with me. However, no matter how willing and eager we were to take on the transition, we were both mostly unaware of the irreversible changes that lay ahead. We experienced changes to each of us individually, changes to our marriage, immense growth in each of our capacity to experience more love, honesty, closeness and pleasure, as well as all the changes that resulted from significant losses, heartbreaks and attachment alterations within our own relationship and with family, friends and other partners. At that time there was nothing in the non-monogamy self-help genre that could fully prepare us for everything our attachment systems were going through, and like many polyamorous couples we had to forge our own path forward, repeatedly stumbling along the way and learning retrospectively at the expense of ourselves, each other and our other partners.

Nothing about my personal journey, professional experiences or transition from monogamy to polyamory has been linear. Unexpectedly, my therapy clients served as my personal catalyst to claiming my own polyamory, which then led me to specialize in working with people practicing nonmonogamy as my primary professional focus. Today, approximately 75 percent of my clients are nonmonogamous, and when I'm not working with clients in person or long distance, I spend my professional time speaking and leading workshops on nonmonogamous relationships, trauma, attachment and transformation.

Why a Book on Nonmonogamy and Attachment?

Romantic relationships in Western society are still fraught with prescriptions and restrictions that inhibit nontradi-tional expressions of love, and many of us suffer greatly from this. As the landscape of romantic love continues to expand and monogamy is no longer the only possible course of action that a relationship can take, our societal notions, as well as our psychological models of love and partnership, also need to grow and include relationship structures beyond the monogamous norm.

Attachment theory offers an important—even revolutionary—framework for understanding the biological and psychological necessity of being securely bonded to others. The psychological model also allows insight into how disruptions in attachment can create significant challenges in the giving and receiving of the love and affection we so desire with our partners. Research has consistently demonstrated that understanding our different attachment styles and using this knowledge to move into more secure functioning with a partner is an important component in creating fulfilling and sustaining relationships. Attachment theory was developed in the 1960s by British psychologist John Bowlby,[2] but in the past several years, it has expanded its reach outside of the academic and therapeutic spheres, becoming more popularized in general public discourse regarding personal healing, parenting, dating, marriages and relationships.

Many people who practice ethical nonmonogamy (who often proudly describe themselves as *relationship geeks*) have been drawn to attachment theory as a way to further enhance their general knowledge about relationships. The theory is also more specifically used to support nonmonogamous people in comprehending and working with the distinct challenges and patterns that arise when someone has multiple partners. While therapeutic practices based on attachment theory have become some of the most effective and well-researched modalities for couples therapy, how it applies to nonmonogamous relationships can be unclear. To no surprise, the majority of resources and advice available on how to create securely attached romantic relationships assume monogamy. Whether intentionally or not, these resources encourage highly mononormative practices, often leaving people who are nonmonogamous at a loss in how to create secure bonds with their multiple partners.

Several years ago, I was in a polyamorous relationship with a partner named Corey. At that time, I lived with my husband and our child, and Corey lived in a nearby town with his primary partner. One day Corey admitted to having an anxious attachment style. We both wanted our relationship to be a close and connected one, but we also knew that living together and blending our families was not in the cards for us, so we began to wonder how we could establish more secure functioning together without the boost in security that comes from either living with a partner, being primaries, sharing finances or having a child together.

We began to listen to an audio version of one of the better books on attachment, eagerly jumping ahead to the section instructing us on the specific things we could do to build secure attachment in our romantic relationship. Being someone who is a minority in several areas of my life, I was already habitually accustomed to having to reinterpret information and advice, automatically translating the typical normative discourses in whatever I was reading to garner any and all kernels of wisdom that I could actually apply to my own life. Corey, however, was not used to having to code switch like this. Taking a more literal read on the chapter, he was left discouraged and concluded that he and I would never achieve secure attachment since we were unable to do over half of the suggested attachment behaviors. I was initially surprised by this because when I read the very same section I had been hopeful. When I paused to consider why I had such a different take on the very same chapter, I realized that my optimism didn't actually come from the author's encouragement, but because I was quick to sift the useful from the useless and the relevant from the irrelevant to our nonmonogamous context. But Corey's perspective was illuminating for me because he was right—if we couldn't do the majority of the advised activities, what were we really left with?

Around the same time, several of my nonmonogamous clients also began expressing similar grievances. Like me and Corey, they wanted secure attachment with *all* of their partners, but they felt demoralized and even pathologized when they read about attachment. They were unable to find themselves or fit themselves into the mononormativity of the literature on attachment, since they were unable to partake in many of the behaviors that experts recommend as required for secure relationships. Even though I was able to translate, sift through and reframe what I was reading from the mainstream books and audio programs in order to apply it to my polyamorous relationships and nonmonogamous clients, I realized that this didn't mean that others—even highly intelligent others like Corey or my clients—could or would do the same. And they shouldn't have to, because secure attachment is not just for the monogamous. So, I took on Corey's and my clients' understandable discouragement as a personal and professional challenge. I promised Corey that I would at least come up with a list of things that we *could* do to cultivate a secure attachment that didn't require us to live together, be exclusive or even be each other's primary partner. That list led into a talk, which has since led to this book. Thank you, Corey! Thank you, clients!

Many nonmonogamous people have secure, loving, healthy relationships with multiple partners, and this book is my attempt at lifting the lens of monogamy from attachment research so that we can apply all this wonderful knowledge about human connection and bonding to a nonmonogamous context. As far as my editors and I know, this is the first book to explicitly translate the principles of attachment theory to nonmonogamous relationships.

Part One covers an overview of attachment theory and trauma. In Chapter One, I offer a general description of attachment theory and how different childhood experiences relate to the four different attachment styles that people can develop. Chapter Two explores some aspects of attachment that are less commonly discussed in the mainstream attachment literature. Here we take a look at the different dimensions of attachment anxiety and attachment avoidance as a more precise way to understand the four different attachment styles. I also reframe the attachment styles based on their strengths and desires (not just their dysfunctions), highlighting how insecure attachment styles can also be expressions of the healthy drives for autonomy and connection. I also discuss the importance of the relationship between attachment styles, boundaries and the giving and receiving of love. In Chapter Three, I present the nested model of attachment and trauma, which I developed to further expand the ways in which we conceive of and discuss attachment and trauma. Attachment and trauma occur over multiple levels or dimensions of our human experience, and here I explore these different levels and how they relate to attachment and trauma.

Part Two looks at the interaction of nonmonogamy and attachment. In Chapter Four, I explain the different reasons why people engage in nonmonogamy and describe the different types of nonmonogamy based on where people identify their level of sexual exclusivity or non-sexual exclusivity intersecting with how emotionally exclusive or emotionally non-exclusive they are. Chapter Five reviews what the current attachment research says about nonmonogamy, and I share my critique of attachment theory from a nonmonogamous perspective. In Chapter Six, I present the observations and insights into nonmonogamy and attachment that I've gained from my therapeutic and coaching practice. At the end of this chapter I apply the nested model of attachment and trauma to illustrate some of the specific and unique ways that people who practice nonmonogamy experience attachment ruptures and trauma at each of the different levels.

Part Three switches modes into a more practical look at what you and your partners can do to cultivate secure attachment in attachment-based polyamorous relationships. Chapter Seven asks you to get clear about whether or not you are on board for attachment-based relationships and then covers what being a *safe haven* and *secure base* might look like for you and your partners. Chapters Eight and Nine guide you through the HEARTS of being polysecure—this acronym articulates six specific things you can do to cultivate secure attachment in your multiple relationships. Chapter Eight focuses on the HEART in HEARTS, looking at how you can enhance your attachment security within and among your relationships, and Chapter Nine focuses on having secure attachment with yourself, an imperative and often overlooked aspect of attachment that I find crucial for nonmonogamy. The book closes with Chapter Ten, where I answer some frequently asked questions and offer my parting words. It is my hope that this book will offer a broader alternative perspective on the application of attachment theory and that as more and more people move forward into the

frontiers of nonmonogamy, these mostly uncharted territories will be traversed ethically, lovingly, skillfully and,
of course, securely.

Part *One*

The first section of this book provides an overview of attachment theory, the four secure and insecure attachment styles, the different dimensions of attachment, and the nested model of attachment and trauma. The descriptions of the different attachment styles used in this book have been adapted from and inspired by the work of Diane Poole Heller, Daniel Siegel, Lisa Firestone, Daniel P. Brown, Mario Mikulincer and Phillip R. Shaver.

Part One

CHAPTER ONE

AN OVERVIEW OF ATTACHMENT THEORY

HEALTHY ATTACHMENT IS A DEEP BOND and an enduring emotional closeness that connects people to one another across space and time.[3] As human infants, we are born into this world with an attachment system that wires us to expect connection with others. The creator of attachment theory, John Bowlby, called this innate expectation the *attachment behavioral system* and explained that it is one of several behavioral systems that humans evolved to ensure our survival. As infants, we can't yet meet any of our own needs. So, in order to survive, we have to bond and attach to caretakers who can provide us with food and shelter, as well as meeting our biological and psychological needs for emotional attunement, warm responsiveness and calming physical touch. Popular parenting culture often calls this "skin time," and it's known to be a crucial part of early childhood development.

When an infant feels fear, distress or discomfort, their attachment system is activated. This prompts them to quickly turn towards their caretakers or use proximity-seeking behaviors such as crying, reaching for, calling out or, later, crawling and following their attachment figure.

All these behaviors are attempts to restore feelings of safety, and in many cases to restore actual safety, too. If the child receives the support, reassurance and comfort they need from their caretaker, their nervous system then returns to a state of calm homeostasis. Infants and children who can't yet fully regulate their own emotional states depend on their caretakers to co-regulate for them. Being close with another human helps children to feel calm. Further, being connected to and soothed by their caretakers over time teaches them how to self-soothe and regulate their own emotional states. As children, we want to know that our attachment figures are nearby and accessible. We need to know that they will provide us with a safe haven to turn to when we need them, which then gives us a secure base from which we can explore our environment. Bowlby called this the *exploratory behavioral system*. When our attachment needs are being met, this system enables us to feel comfortable and free to explore ourselves, others and the world around us.

John Bowlby and Mary Ainsworth's research shows that children develop attachment styles that are more secure or more insecure, depending on how well their parents are able to be a connected and responsive safe haven for them. If their caretakers are able to meet most of their needs enough of the time, children usually have a secure attachment. But if they experience their parents as inconsistent, inaccessible, unresponsive or even threatening and dangerous, they adapt by developing more insecure attachment styles. If our attachment figures were absent or scary to us as children, we didn't develop our ability to freely explore and to learn about the world and about our own abilities. When this happens, we develop insecure strategies for engaging with others—we may become more vigilant and anxious or more avoidant and dismissive.

Mikulincer and Shaver created a model of attachment-system functioning and dynamics,[4] which I've adapted into a flowchart showing how the different attachment experiences arise. First, if a child experiences a threat—whether perceived or actual, physical or emotional—they will try to find protection by seeking closeness to an attachment figure. If their attachment figure is available and responsive, and meets their needs, the child feels safe and can go back to playing or exploring. But if their attachment figure is unresponsive or inaccessible, and the child is left without a safe haven to turn to, they may adapt by either *deactivating* (turning down) or *hyperactivating* (turning up) their attachment needs.

As children, when we feel afraid, threatened or in need, and seeking closeness with our parents is *not* a viable option because they're not available or because turning towards them doesn't make things better, we learn to rely more on ourselves. We become more self-reliant and we minimize our attachment needs. When we deactivate our attachment system, we suppress our attachment-based longings—not because we don't still want closeness and connection, but in order to adapt and survive. If we experience discomfort or danger and closeness to a parent is still *somewhat* of a viable option, we might learn that we can get their attention by inten-sifying our attachment cries. If our caretakers did not respond to our initial bids, but ramping up our demands and hyperactivating our attachment system did get their attention in some form, we then learn that this is an effective strategy. Later in this chapter, we'll talk about how these strategies—deactivating, hyperactivating, or vacillating between the two—relate to the three different insecure attachment styles.

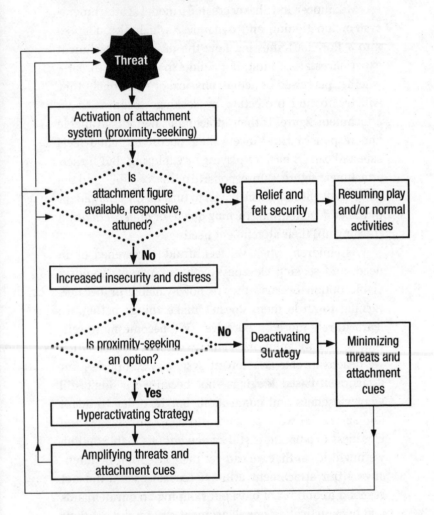

FIGURE 1.1 An adaptation of Mikulincer and Shaver's model of attachment-system activation and functioning in adulthood.[5]

Caregiver behaviors that could lead a child to take on a deactivating attachment strategy include:
- Neglecting or abusing the child.
- Being emotionally cold or rejecting the child.
- Giving the child hostile, angry or threatening responses.
- Discouraging a child's expression of vulnerability.
- Encouraging (whether explicitly or implicitly) the child to be more self-reliant and independent.

Caregiver behaviors that can incite hyperactivating attachment strategies include:
- Being unreliable, unpredictable or intrusive, where interactions are sometimes gratifying and connected, but at other times mis-attuned and disconnected.
- Punishing or criticizing a child for their independence or curiosity.
- Conveying messages that the child is not enough, or is incapable, stupid or failing in some way.
- Taking on a helicopter style of parenting, which might include excessive praise but also excessive control, protectiveness or perfectionism.
- Experiences of abuse or traumas that occur when the child is separated from their primary attachment figure, which can reinforce the notion that it's dangerous to be apart from them.

Both of these strategies can also occur simultaneously, meaning a child may experience both hyperactivation and deactivation, or may vacillate between the two survival strategies. We'll discuss this more in the section about fearful-avoidant attachment.

Secure Attachment: When Attachment Needs Are Met in Childhood

Children who have a secure attachment style have generally experienced a family environment that's mostly warm and supportive. Their parents or caretakers are available, accessible and responsive to their needs, enough of the time. Not necessarily *all* of the time but *enough of the time*, when the child has an attachment need, they reach out to their attachment figure and that attachment figure moves towards them in an emotionally attuned way that calms the child's nervous system.[6] This in turn teaches the child that allowing themselves to feel their needs and communicating those needs to others is an effective strategy. A caretaker being present, safe, protective, playful, emotionally attuned and responsive is of paramount importance to a child developing a secure attachment style.

Early positive attachment experiences have a huge impact on healthy brain development and emotional regulation.[7] When the attachment figure is able to emotionally resonate with the child, the child feels supported and learns to regulate their own positive and negative emotional arousal. This helps to lower stress hormones and increase oxytocin (the bonding hormone). By co-regulating with a caretaker, the child learns to understand and process facial and social cues, they learn empathy and they develop an increased ability to cope with stress. When children experience secure interactions with the adults in their lives and function from a secure attachment style, they also tend to have better self-esteem, be more resilient to trauma, have strong social skills, concentrate better, enjoy play and have solid overall emotional health.

Through these nourishing experiences, a child develops a sense of safety and trust. They take in the messages that the world is a friendly place and that they can ask for what they want because the people in their lives care and are willing to help.

Secure Attachment as an Adult

Early childhood attachment experiences become the blueprint for the kinds of connections we go on to expect and seek in our adult romantic relationships. The interactions we experienced with our caretakers create internal working models of how we see ourselves—both positively and negatively—and set our positive or negative expectations about how attuned and available our partners will be to us in times of need.[8] People with a secure attachment style experience a healthy sense of self and see themselves and their partners in a positive light. Their interpersonal experiences are deeply informed by their knowledge that they can ask for what they need and people will typically listen and willingly respond. It's empowering to know that our actions are effective. As children, if we reach out with our body and use our voice to get the help or connection we need to mitigate our distress, and if our parents usually meet these attachment bids, we learn that we matter and are worthy of love. This builds the foundation for healthy self-esteem and a sense of competence in the world. As adults, this helps us be more flexible when our partners can't meet our needs. We're better able to weather hearing no, to wait for our needs to be met at a later time or to seek an alternative means of having our attachment needs met without shaking the foundation of our relationship.

Bowlby viewed attachment as relevant "from the cradle to the grave."[9] He said that adult romantic relationships function as reciprocal attachment bonds, where each partner serves as an attachment figure for the other. Bowlby conceived of the parent-child attachment relationship as having four essential features: *proximity maintenance, separation distress, safe haven* and *secure base*. We can see many parallels between the parent-child attachment relationship and the adult-adult attachment relationship. For instance, adults seek physical contact with each other, engage in dreamy eye-gazing, and even use baby talk or cooing sounds to nurture and encourage bonding. We feel separation distress when apart, and we turn towards our romantic partners as a safe haven in times of need. We also see them as a secure base from which to explore the world and our sexuality, and we feel able to share important discoveries with them.[10]

Of course, there are differences between the parent-child attachment bond and the adult-adult attachment bond. As adults, even though we seek regular and consistent proximity to our partner, we can tolerate much longer periods of separation from our partners by employing mental representations of them to help give us an understanding of why we are apart (e.g., "I know my partner is at work," "My partner is away on a trip" or "I have this weekend with my kids and I'll see my partner in a few days"). As adults, we are also better equipped than children to leverage positive fantasies about our partner; we can imagine what it will feel like when we're reunited, and we can access a bodily felt sense of their presence, which can offer reassurances of comfort and security when physically apart.

Two additional changes in adult attachment compared to parent-child attachment include mutual caregiving and sexuality.[11] As children, caregiving is asymmetrical: a child under secure circumstances receives care from their attachment figures but does not provide it in return. But as adults, caretaking becomes more symmetrical and shared between partners. Sexuality also becomes an integrated part of the attachment and caregiving behavioral systems.

A child with a secure attachment style will likely grow up into an adult who feels worthy of love and seeks to create meaningful, healthy relationships with people who are physically and emotionally available. Securely functioning adults are comfortable with intimacy, closeness, and their need or desire for others. They don't fear losing their sense of self or being engulfed by the relationship. For securely attached people, "dependency" is not a dirty word, but a fact of life that can be experienced without losing or compromising the self.

Conversely, securely functioning adults are also comfortable with their independence and personal autonomy. They may miss their partners when they're not together, but inside they feel fundamentally alright with themselves when they're alone. They also feel minimal fear of abandonment when temporarily separated from their partner. In other words, securely attached people experience *relational object constancy*, which is the ability to trust in and maintain an emotional bond with people even during physical or emotional separation.

Object constancy is a developmental milestone where a child is able to understand that their attachment figure is a separate person. This person can love and be there for them, but they can leave the room and, even if they're temporarily out of sight, it doesn't mean they're completely gone. In adulthood, relational object constancy enables us to trust that our connections and bonds with people will endure even if we're apart. People with secure attachment are able to internalize their partners' love, carrying it with them even when they're physically separate, emotionally disconnected or in conflict.

Another important aspect of secure attachment is that, when distressed, a person can both emotionally regulate on their own, and can also co-regulate and receive support from their partners. People functioning from a securely attached style are better able to take care of their own needs as well as ask their partners to help out. In my psychotherapy practice, I've noticed that more securely attached partners are often better able to set healthy boundaries. They truly say no when they mean no and yes when they mean yes. To me, this is the foundation of true consent.

Research has also shown that having a secure attachment style as an adult is correlated with higher levels of relationship satisfaction and balance,[12] higher levels of empathy, respect and forgiveness for partners,[13] and higher levels of sexual satisfaction when compared to people who are insecurely attached in their relationships.[14] Additionally, having a secure base with a partner can increase *sexploration*, a term coined to describe "the degree to which a person co-constructs a sex-positive, supportive, and safe environment with their partner(s)."[15] If you've been to one of my talks on attachment, you will have heard me say that secure attachment is the new sexy!

Statements that someone with a secure attachment style might make:

- I find it easy to make emotional connections with others.
- I enjoy being close with others.
- I am comfortable depending on others and having others depend on me.
- I don't often worry about being abandoned or about someone getting too close to me.
- If I am in distress I can easily turn to my attachment figure for comfort and support.
- I am aware and accepting of my partners' strengths and shortcomings, and I treat them with love and respect.
- During conflict or disagreement, I am able to take responsibility for my part, apologize when needed, clear up misunderstandings, apply problem-solving strategies and forgive when needed.
- I do well with the transition of going from being by myself to then being together with a partner, and I also do well with the transition of going from being together to then being alone again.

When Attachment Needs Are Not Met

So far, I've described the optimal situations for attachment in childhood and then adulthood—but approximately half the time, this ideal is far from achieved, leading to the three different expressions of insecure attachment: avoidant, anxious and disorganized. In general, with these three different insecure styles, regardless of what specific insecure adaptations a child develops, they will go on to have difficulty with certain relational skills and personal capacities. A person with any of the insecure styles will usually struggle with regulating their own emotional states in healthy ways. They may deactivate, suppress or deny their emotions, or they may hyperactivate and inflame their emotions, and be easily taken over by emotional states.

We learn how to self-regulate through our connections with our attachment figures. So, if our parents were unable to regulate their own emotions (whether from their current stress levels or their previous unresolved trauma), and therefore couldn't support us in regulating our own emotions, we lost a foundational developmental experience. In the absence of the foundational neuropsychological experience of receiving soothing and emotional regulation from our parents, as adults we then have to learn these difficult developmental tasks on our own. We have to figure out how to identify and articulate our emotional states and then find ways to self-soothe as a healthy response instead of pulling away, shutting down or lashing out in emotional reactivity. We also need to learn how to healthily rely on others and to figure out when it's appropriate to seek support from them to help regulate our emotions.

Children who experienced an insecure attachment environment, regardless of which style they adopted, can internalize the beliefs that to some degree the world is unsafe and people cannot truly be relied on. These children will also struggle with having a sturdy relational object constancy. Since relational object constancy is the ability to trust that your connection and bond with someone will persist beyond an initial separation or conflict, as an adult, having a compromised relational object constancy can make it extremely difficult to get through the disappointments, uncertainties, healthy conflicts, and natural ebbs and flows that adult romantic relationships inevitably produce. Research also demonstrates that people with insecure attachment styles in adulthood struggle with relationship satisfaction.[16] They find it hard to trust their partners, forgive them and respond intentionally instead of reacting out of habit. They also face challenges when it comes to commitment, whether they tend to commit too soon or not commit at all.

A Caveat to the Attachment Styles

Before you read the next section, which describes the three different insecure styles, there are several important points that I'd like for you to keep in mind.

- Attachment wounds can occur for many reasons, and it is imperative to emphasize that attachment ruptures are not always the fault of one's attachment figures. Attachment theory is not about parent blaming. Disruptions in attachment can occur for various reasons outside of the attachment figures' control: physical or mental illness, hospitalizations, accidents, the needs of other children or family members in the home, death, poverty, housing instability, war and other social factors. I give a more in-depth analysis of the different levels of potential attachment ruptures in Chapter Three.
- Attachment styles are *not* static! If you experienced an insecurely attached childhood you can still go on to have healthy securely attached adult

relationships, experiencing what is called an *earned secure attachment*. Your attachment styles are survival adaptations to your environment and since they were learned, they can also be unlearned. I will touch more on earned secure attachment in Part Three.

- Attachment styles are not rigid identities to take on. These different insecure styles are not how you relate all of the time and they are not the totality of who you are. I often hear people describe themselves as "I *am* an avoidant" or "I *am* anxiously attached," seeing themselves wholly through this one lens. We can also do this to our partners, labeling them and everything they do as a result of them "being an avoidant" or "being preoccupied," etc.

- From a narrative therapy perspective, this would be a form of essentializing in which someone takes one part of their identity or experience and sees it as the entirety of who they are. To me, this also exposes the paradox of labels. Labeling ourselves or even receiving a diagnosis can be very helpful. It can give important clarity and definition to the struggles that we have been facing. Whether it be a personality type, a medical condition, a psychiatric diagnosis or an astrology chart, finding ourselves in a certain *type* can be refreshing. We may feel that our experience is no longer mysterious or just limited to us, but is actually understood, well-articulated and even shared with others. For some, reading about a certain attachment style can literally put their entire life and relationship history into context, liberating them from the idea that they are broken or helplessly doomed to never have relationship success. Instead, they can see themselves as a person who has wisely taken on a certain attachment adaptation and they can feel empowered to change that adaptation and choose a more secure path from which to move forward.

Conversely, labeling or receiving a diagnosis can also confine us into rigid categories that may restrict our sense of self or obscure the fullness of who we are. Labels can easily keep us stuck in the mindset of *this is who I am, and so this is who I will continue to be*. Instead of seeing ourselves as someone who struggles with anxiety, we see ourselves as anxiety itself. Instead of seeing ourselves as someone who is battling depression, we see ourselves as depression itself. So, when reading about attachment styles, please identify with what feels useful, and please be mindful of rigidly identifying yourself or others. We are more than the problems we face.

- You might relate to more than one style. Some people see themselves in two, three or even all four of the styles. You might function from a more secure style most of the time, but then act out a particular insecure style while under stress, or you might experience different attachment styles depending on who you are relating to. Many of us have different attachment styles in relation to each of our parents, for example—we might have felt very secure with one parent, but insecure with another. The styles of our partners also have an impact on our own attachment expression. A partner with a dismissive attachment style might

provoke more anxious/preoccupied behaviors
from us, or being with a more anxious partner
might polarize us into being more dismissive. Our
attachment styles can change from one relationship to the next and they can also change within a
specific relationship with the same person.

- Lastly, your attachment style is not an excuse for
abuse! I've heard people use their attachment
style as an excuse for their actions, blaming their
unskilled or even harmful behaviors on the "fact"
of them having a certain attachment style. Please
don't do this! If you are acting out in harmful ways
towards yourself, your partners or anyone you're
in contact with, please take your traumas and
wounds seriously and seek professional support.
Cycles of violence, abuse or neglect can undoubtedly be broken when the right support is in place.

Insecure Attachment Styles

In this section, I will first present the three insecure styles
in the typology in which they are commonly presented by
other authors. However, some researchers and theorists
have moved away from using the traditional four-type
attachment typology, proposing instead that attachment
plays out over the two dimensions of *attachment anxiety* and *attachment avoidance*. This two-dimensional
perspective can be a more precise way of understanding
the different expressions of the secure and insecure
attachment styles, which I will present after the three
insecure styles.

The Avoidant/Dismissive Attachment Style

Avoidant Attachment in Childhood

The avoidant and anxious styles were first observed in children by Mary Ainsworth in 1978 through her Strange Situation Procedure.[17] In these experiments, infants and young children were observed with their primary attachment figure (usually the mother) in a room filled with toys. Each child was at times alone with their parent in the room, then left alone with a stranger while the parent stepped out of the room for several minutes. Of particular interest were how much the child explored the room of toys, how much anxiety the child felt when left alone with the stranger and how the child responded to first being separated and then reunited with their parent. The child's response to separation and reunion became the primary way of assessing secure and insecure attachment.

Children with a secure attachment were observed as comfortable exploring the room of toys while their parents were present, at ease interacting with strangers when parents were present and then expressing healthy attachment distress when their parents left the room, followed by relief and comfort when their parents returned.

The children who were classified with the avoidant attachment pattern were observed as being distant from their caretakers, showing little to no distress upon separation, expressing little interest in the parents upon reunion, and even showing little preference for being with their parents versus the stranger. These children were less likely to explore the room of toys and often preferred to play by themselves. Interestingly, the seemingly unaffected demeanor of these children, who were physically and emotionally distant from their caretakers, did not reflect their internal state. Even though these children appeared "fine" on the outside, they were actually experiencing internal signs of elevated heart rate and physiological stress.

A child who had parents who were mostly unavailable, neglectful or absent adapted to their attachment environment by taking on a more avoidant style. Parenting that is cold, distant, critical or highly focused on achievement or appearance can create an environment where the child learns that they are better off relying on themselves. When a child does not get enough of the positive attachment responses that they need or they are outright rejected or criticized for having needs, they will adapt by shutting down and deactivating their attachment longings. A child in this scenario learns that, in order to survive, they need to inhibit their attachment bids for proximity or protection in order to prevent the pain and confusion of neglect or rejection. In this situation a child often learns to subsist on emotional crumbs, assuming that the best way to get their needs met by their parent is to act as if they don't have any. In adulthood, having a deactivated attachment system includes not only minimizing one's own bids for care and attention, but also having a diminished ability to pick up on and register attachment cues from others.

Some of the different factors that can contribute to a child adopting an avoidant attachment style are:[18]

- Isolation through too much time alone or not enough face-to-face time with parents.
- The absence of physical or emotional presence from caretakers.

- Too much emphasis on task-based presence. That is, where caregivers are only present when they are trying to educate or teach something to their child that is practical, academic or skills-based.
- Too little touch and affection, or what Diane Poole Heller calls "skin hunger."
- Emotional neglect where emotional nourishment is low or absent and parents are unable to effectively read the child's signals. Such parents might respond in insensitive ways or be completely unresponsive to the child's emotional states and needs.
- Expressive dissonance, which is when someone's facial or verbal expressions are mismatched with their emotional states. Someone might be laughing when they are angry or smiling when they are actually upset, which can be confusing to children (or anyone for that matter). Since children are learning how to identify and express their own emotional states through the modeling of the adults around them, a parent with expressive dissonance can create challenges in their child's ability to understand others' feelings and to express themselves in ways that are socially appropriate and authentic.
- Disrupted engagement with caretakers due to illnesses or other factors that interfere with either the child or the parent participating in bonding attachment behaviors (see the nested attachment model in Chapter Three).
- Rejection from parents that might be ongoing, subtle or even outright abandonment of the child and parental responsibilities.
- Parents who are overly strict and controlling.

- Parents who might have the best intentions, but have a child who is so different from them that they are unable to understand or connect with that child in attuned ways.

Dismissive Attachment as an Adult

In adulthood, the childhood avoidant style is referred to as dismissive. A person who is functioning from a dismissive style will tend to keep people at arm's length. Usually priding themselves on not needing anyone, people with this style will tend to take on an overly self-reliant outlook, valuing their hyper-independence and often seeing others as weak, needy or too dependent. Although they may present as having high self-esteem, people functioning from a dismissive attachment style often project unwanted traits onto others and inflate their sense of self to cover a relatively negative self-image. People with this attachment style have reported lower levels of relationship satisfaction, trust and commitment,[19] as well as having more negative views about sex and lower levels of sexual satisfaction when married.[20]

A person with a dismissive attachment style likely didn't get what they needed early in life from their primary caregivers, so they learned to get by and survive by needing little to nothing from others. When someone grows up in a home with minimal or no emotional nourishment, it makes sense that they would deemphasize the value and importance of relationships, and that they find it extremely difficult to be vulnerable and open with others. Oftentimes, their own painful emotions or experiences are placed below the radar of their emotional awareness in order to avoid the discomfort of feeling pain. This in turn creates a disconnection from their own feelings and needs. Living with a sense of chronic disconnection from themselves, others and the world, they might at times experience the longing to be close, but then feel at a total loss as to how to bridge the gap between their isolation and others, missing opportunities to receive support from their partners or to provide care to their loved ones.

People in this attachment style *do* want relationships. They will enter into relationships, even long-term relationships, but may struggle with their ability to reflect on their own internal experience as well as sensitively respond to the signals of their partners. They usually find it difficult to tolerate emotions related to intimacy, conflict and different forms of emotional intensity. When someone who is functioning in this style either feels vulnerable or perceives vulnerability in their partner, they will distance themselves to avoid discomfort. Signs of potential rejection or criticism from others will also create a quick withdrawal.

People with the dismissive attachment style will also tend to be highly linear and logical, showing many forms of competence and ability in the practical or professional realms of life. This overdevelopment of the logical brain can also create challenges with certain aspects of autobiographical memory—people with a dismissive attachment style might have little memory for childhood experiences, as well as simplistic narratives about their parents and childhood being "just fine."[21]

In my therapy practice, I often notice that people who are relating from the dismissive style initially describe their parents or current romantic relationships as being great, even ideal, but just a few minutes of deeper questioning into their actual childhood experiences or current

relational patterns reveals that things aren't actually so
perfect. This occurs because the deactivation of their
attachment system has made it difficult for them to access
and consistently stay in touch with their true feelings.
For many, contacting and admitting one's actual feelings
might be perceived as a threat to their current relationship or to the status quo of their family of origin.

Part of this deactivating and distancing adaptation
is the dissociation from lived experience. When someone
with a dismissive style starts to work on healing their
insecure attachment, they must begin by no longer dismissing and distancing from themselves. This requires
that they no longer deny their desires and needs, allowing
the longings and wants for connection that have for so
long been forbidden. When someone functioning from a
dismissive style starts to allow their attachment system
to come back online, it can initially be a very tender, raw
and even overwhelming process. The skills that come
with being able to identify your own feelings are part of
a developmental process that takes time. The process of
allowing feelings as they arise, learning how to self-soothe
and establishing an inner trust that experiencing feelings
is safe, cannot be rushed.

For the dismissive style, the journey from insecure to
secure attachment is one of returning to the body through
bringing feelings and sensations back to life and learning how to be with oneself in this process. Once this is
established, the risk of then leaning into others, revealing
one's internal world, and dismantling the self-reliant
exoskeleton through asking for help and care from others
can begin.

Statements that someone with a dismissive attachment style might make:

- My autonomy, independence and self-sufficiency are very important to me.
- I am generally comfortable without close relationships and do well on my own.
- I want to be in relationships and have some closeness with people, but I can only tolerate closeness to a limit and then I need space.
- I prefer not to share my feelings or show a partner how I feel deep down.
- I frequently don't know what I'm feeling or needing and/or I can miss cues from others about what they are feeling or needing.
- I feel uncomfortable relying on partners and having partners depend or rely on me.
- I either struggle with making relationship commitments or if I do commit, I may secretly have one foot out the door (or at least have the back door unlocked).
- I am very sensitive to any signs that my partner is trying to control me or interfere with my freedom in any way (and I don't like the word "sensitive").
- I see myself or others as weak for having needs or wanting comfort, help or reassurance.
- During disagreements or in conflict I tend to withdraw, shut down, shut out or stonewall.
- I do well with the transition from being together with people to then being alone again, but once I've been alone for a while I can be slow to warm up to others or struggle with the transition from being alone to entering back into connection with someone.

The Anxious/Preoccupied Attachment Style

Anxious Attachment in Childhood

In Ainsworth's Strange Situation Procedure, children who were classified as being anxiously attached were reluctant to play with the toys in the room even when their parent was present. They showed signs of distress and clinginess even before their parent left the room and struggled to settle down upon reunion with their caregiver. For these children, the attachment system was hyperactivated, in comparison to the deactivating of the attachment system that the avoidant style employs. Hyperactivating the attachment system ramps up the desire for a caretaker, amplifying the child's attachment bids as a way to capture a parent's attention.

Parents who are loving but inconsistent can encourage the adaptation of the anxious style. Sometimes the parent is here and available, attuned and responsive, but then other times they are emotionally unavailable, misattuned or even intrusive, leaving the child confused and uncertain as to whether their parent is going to comfort them, ignore them, reward them or punish them for the very same behavior. This unpredictability can be very dysregulating for a child who is trying to stabilize a bond with their caregiver so, in an attempt to cope, they then learn that hyperactivating their attachment system through getting louder or needier achieves the attention they need. In this scenario, the child can become dependent on their hyperactivating strategy in order to survive, fearing that if they let their attachment system settle and rest then their needs will never be met. This in turn can lead to a chronically activated attachment system that exaggerates threats of potential abandonment, which may or may not actually be there.[22]

Some factors that can contribute to a child adopting an anxious insecure attachment style are:[23]

- Parents who are unable to consistently co-regulate with their child, which leaves the child dependent on others to regulate their emotions, again and again turning outward to make sense of their inner feelings and unable to emotionally regulate on their own.

- Over-involving the child in the parent's state of mind, where the parent's emotions or state of mind is more central to the parent-child interaction than the child's. In this case, the child might be asked (whether explicitly or implicitly) to be responsible for meeting the parent's needs, making the parent feel better or supplying the parent with meaning and purpose. This is often due to a parent's own level of anxiety, stress or unresolved trauma, or their own anxious attachment history. When the state of mind of the parent is the centerpiece of interactions, the child is left to constantly monitor and be concerned about their parent's state of well-being, which can encourage a role reversal in which the child is acting more like the parent in the relationship. As a child, being responsible for a parent's well-being is a mis-placed, confusing and overwhelming responsibility.

- Overstimulation. We live in an increasingly stim-ulating world, with fewer spaces to rest physically and mentally between interactions with people, technology, billboards, ads and the like. Our nervous systems need breaks from such stimulation in order to develop properly, and parents can impede this process when they force constant contact, require attention or presence from a child that might be beyond their developmental capacity, hover over the child, interject themselves when the child is calmly playing independently or enjoying time with others, or even push physical boundaries through tickling or affection that is unwanted by the child in that particular moment.

- Parents who discourage autonomy. Some parents discourage their child's agency and autonomy through comments or suggestions that insinuate, whether subtly or overtly, that the child is incapable, less than or not enough in some way. Even well-intentioned parents can question their children's actions and decisions in ways that are shaming instead of encouraging. Some parents who are struggling with their own anxiety can easily get overwhelmed by children who want to explore and discourage or overprotect the child in ways that undermine their interests or abilities.

Preoccupied Attachment as an Adult

When used to characterize an adult, anxious attachment is called preoccupied. People with this attachment style demonstrate an intense focus and heightened concern about the level of closeness in their relationships. A defining factor of the preoccupied style is how the person's hyperactivated attachment strategy not only amplifies their attachment bids, but also intensifies their focus on their partners. Because of this, they may end up constantly monitoring their partners' level of availability, interest and responsiveness. The partner of someone with a preoccupied attachment style may then feel like this constant tracking of relational mis-attunements and mistakes is controlling of them. But for the person with a preoccupied attachment style, this behavior is less an attempt to overtly control their partner than it is a symptom of their attachment system being overly sensitive to even the slightest sign they might be left. From their perspective, they're not trying to control their partner; they're just grasping for a relationship they're afraid is slipping out of their hands.

Hyperfocus on the other can lead to a disconnection or loss of self through over-functioning and over-adapting in the relationship in an attempt to maintain and preserve the connection. Frequently consumed by fears of abandonment, people functioning out of a preoccupied style will easily give up their own needs or sense of self, yielding to the needs or identity of their partner in order to ensure proximity and relationship security. Due to their history of unpredictable and inconsistent love, they can have considerable challenges with trusting that their partners truly love them. They may frequently fall into self-critical and self-doubting loops, questioning if they are truly worthy enough to receive their partner's love. They often have a hard time fully taking in the love they so desperately want, even when it is given. People functioning from this style tend to jump into relationships or bond very quickly with people. Often idealizing their partners, they may confuse anxiety and intensity for being in love, hearing and seeing only what they want to see and missing potential red flags. They may not allow enough time to get to know someone beyond the honeymoon phase in order to assess if this person, and the relationship, are truly a good fit.

A person with a preoccupied style can be uncomfortable, even terrified, of being alone. They often promote their own dependency on their partners (or they might promote their partners' dependency on them) in a way that discourages doing things separately from each other. Engaging in compulsive caretaking can also become a way to prevent the discomfort of feeling lonely and enhance the perceived security of not being abandoned. Even though people with this style tend to sacrifice themselves for the relationship, the ways in which they are preoccupied and compulsively give care are not necessarily attuned. In such cases, the caregiving is more of a strategy to keep a person close than an actual response to what their partner genuinely needs. If someone with this attachment style perceives even the slightest possibility that their partner is disconnected or disinterested, they can become demanding, possessive or needy for approval, reassurance, connection, contact, and greater emotional or sexual intensity.

From their partner's perspective, the needs of the person with the preoccupied attachment style may seem insatiable. The partner may feel they can never do enough, which can in turn create the very pulling away or even breaking up that the person with the preoccupied style is so desperate to avoid. Compared to people with a more secure attachment style, people with the preoccupied style report increased jealousy and relationship conflict,[24] as well as feelings of ambivalence about their sex life, since they are less likely to use consistent contraception and more likely to engage in sex they don't fully want.[25]

Similar to people with a dismissive attachment adaptation, people with the preoccupied adaptation also have difficulty identifying and describing their own emotions. Initially, this may seem counterintuitive since the preoccupied person is much more emotionally focused, self-disclosing and heightened in both their emotional experience and expression in comparison to someone with a dismissive style, who typically has less access to their feelings. But it makes sense if you look a little closer. Someone with a preoccupied style has more awareness of both their feelings and their partner's feelings, but they still struggle with differentiating and communicating their feelings and with managing their emotional responses in healthy ways. Also, although they're aware of their partner's feelings, they're not necessarily reading those feelings accurately. People with this attachment style might be very precise in detecting even the slightest change in their partner's mood or state, but they're more likely to assume that the shifts are personal to them and that they are negative, when neither may be true.

Part Three covers ways to heal the different attachment styles, and provides a more in-depth look at self-soothing. It also explains a model called HEARTS, which describes secure functioning in ways that can be applied to healing your own attachment challenges. For now, I'll just say that someone with a preoccupied style must first come back to themselves. I will often guide clients to tune into where their sense of self is. Is it within their own body or out there in someone else's body? If it is with someone else, we can then focus on calling themselves back to establish a sense of inner authority and self-trust.

Statements that someone with a preoccupied attachment style might make:

- I am comfortable with connection and usually crave it more than my partners do.
- I am very attuned to others and can detect subtle shifts in their emotional or mental states.

- I often worry about being abandoned, rejected or not valued enough.
- I tend to overfocus on my partners and underfocus on myself.
- When I am going through something, I tend to reach out and turn towards others to make sense of what I'm experiencing or to make myself feel better.
- I need a lot of reassurance that I am loved or desired by a partner; however, when my partners give me reassurance or show their desire for me, it either doesn't register for me or I have trouble receiving and believing it.
- I tend to commit to relationships and get attached very quickly.
- I get frustrated or hurt if a partner is not available when I need them.
- I get resentful or take it personally when a partner spends time away from me.
- I do well with the transition from being alone to being together with partners, but I struggle when going from being together to being alone again.
- I tend to hold on to resentments and have trouble letting go of old wounds.

The Disorganized/Fearful-Avoidant Attachment Style

Disorganized Attachment in Childhood

The final insecure style was not initially classified in Mary Ainsworth's original studies, but was named later by Main and Solomon.[26] Ainsworth observed that a percentage of the children in her Strange Situation Procedure did not neatly fit into one of the three categories of secure, anxious and avoidant. Some children displayed confusing, even chaotic, behaviors such as running towards their parent then immediately away from them, freezing up, hitting their parent for no apparent reason, rolling or throwing themselves on the floor, and more. Main and Solomon later reassessed these findings, and furthered our understanding of the attachment styles by adding the fourth classification of disorganized.

Children with a disorganized attachment style have an attachment system that seems to be hyperactivated and deactivated at the same time. They don't display a consistent organized attachment strategy in the same way that children with a secure, anxious or avoidant style do. Instead, they seemed to lack a coherent organization of which strategy to employ, often vacillating between the anxious and avoidant insecure attachment styles.

The disorganized attachment style is most commonly associated with trauma and it typically arises when a child experiences their attachment figure as scary, threatening or dangerous. When we are afraid, our attachment system gets activated to seek proximity to and comfort from our attachment figure, but what happens when our attachment figure is the person causing the threat? This puts the child in a paradoxical situation where their caretaker, who is supposed to be the source of their comfort and the solution to their fears, is actually the source of their fear instead. Diane Poole Heller refers to this conflicting experience as having *one foot on the gas and one foot on the brake*. The child's attachment system wants to move towards their attachment figure, while the protective defensive mechanism of flight / flight / freeze / appease wants to move away from the attachment figure, and the two systems are coactivated.

The predominant factor leading to this style in childhood is having parents who are suffering from their own unresolved trauma or losses. When a parent has a history of unresolved trauma, they are more easily overwhelmed by life's demands and emotionally flooded by their child's emotional states. Unable to regulate their own emotions, parents with their own history of unhealed trauma, neglect or abuse might then act out, lash out or completely tune out in ways that are scary to the child. Whether that parent is being terrifyingly overresponsive or frighteningly underresponsive, the child learns that they're not safe with the very person who's supposed to protect them. Research has shown that approximately 20 to 40 percent of the general population has some degree of a disorganized attachment style, and approximately 80 percent of children who have experienced abuse develop a disorganized attachment style to one or both of their parents.

Additional factors that can lead to a disorganized attachment style include:[27]

- Parents who are on an emotional roller-coaster. Parents who have drastic, unpredictable fluctuations in their moods, actions or mental states can be extremely confusing for the child, leaving them uncertain whether to approach or withdraw. One of my clients described how her stepmother's emotionally erratic behavior was still lingering in her own nervous system decades later. At family holidays, her stepmother would dote on her one minute, showering her with gifts and praise, and then minutes later would erupt in a yelling fury, shaming her for not paying enough attention to her younger stepbrother. This client recalled how she wasn't the only one who fell into a freeze response when her stepmother had these outbursts; all of the adults in the house did—including her father. They would freeze up, unsure about how to handle the situation. This left her additionally abandoned by the other adults around her, who could have stepped in to mitigate the situation in some way that was responsive and protective for her at a crucial time.

- Parents who are contradictory in their communication. Indirect signals or direct expressions that tell the child to come close but then go away, that they are loved but then unworthy of love, or that they should succeed but are a failure can all be perplexing to a child. Similarly, unrealistic expectations, catch-22s, being punished or shamed for not doing something that they were never shown how to do, being asked to solve problems that are unsolvable, or being expected to do tasks beyond their developmental capability can all lead to a level of disorientation where the child is left frozen and unclear whether to move up or down, right or left. They are damned if they do, damned if they don't.

- Family chaos. Factors such as illness, financial stress, job insecurity, parents who are imprisoned or handling addictions, and even a culture of overachieving in which every minute of a child's life is scheduled with extracurricular activities can all create a home of chaos. It is difficult to feel safe and secure when the home that we live in and the people we rely on are unstable, unpredictable or even erratic. Well-intentioned parents who push their child into more and more enriching activities can cause children to feel destabilized from the lack of rest, downtime and free play time that is needed to feel settled and soothed in the nervous system. In such cases, attachment figures may not be engaging in direct mistreatment of their child, but the surrounding environment or some of the parents' behaviors can create fear and chaos for the child, disrupting their ability to feel safe and secure.

- The child may be a Highly Sensitive Person (HSP) or have a challenging health condition. While disorganized attachment is often associated with parental abuse and neglect, this isn't always the case. Certain traits or experiences specific to the child can also prompt a disorganized experience. Approximately 15 to 20 percent of the population has a nervous system wired to be more sensitive. These people are more attuned to the subtleties of their environment and process that information much more deeply compared to others without this trait.[28] While being more observant might be a survival advantage, it can also be overwhelming. Someone who is constantly aware of the subtleties of the environment and of the people around them can quickly experience sensory overload. My clients who consider themselves to be HSPs often report experiencing a certain type of disorganized attachment because the world itself is too much. Due to their increased sensitivity, even normal everyday events can feel too intense, too chaotic or too stimulating, leaving little respite to feel settled, safe and secure. In relationships, HSPs are often unclear as to whether what they are feeling has its origin in themselves or if their partner's feelings are creating that "one foot on the gas, one foot on the brake" experience in their nervous system. They want to be close to people, but being close can be a sensory assault that is confusing or that dysregulates them for days.

Similarly, I see people with certain illnesses who also suffer with a disorganized attachment, not because of their parental experiences, but because of the world and the body they find themselves in. Imagine what it's like to eat a certain food that may be innocuous for most people, but can spiral you into debilitating physical and mental symptoms for days. Or imagine what it would be like to be invited to a friend's house for their birthday, which should be celebratory, but is actually terrifying to you because you don't know if you are going to be exposed to mold that can set off neurological symptoms that will interfere with your ability to think, walk or talk. Or imagine what it would be like for someone with chemical sensitivities who can't just jump into a taxi, stay in a hotel or even at times walk into a grocery store without experiencing an olfactory punch that can leave them less than functional for days. In such cases, the world itself isn't safe and our bodies are not safe in the world. When autoimmunity is at play, someone will experience a paradoxical situation where the immune system that is supposed to be protecting them is actually harming them and the body that is the vehicle for life is the very thing taking it away.

Fearful-Avoidant Attachment as an Adult

In adulthood, the disorganized attachment style is referred to as fearful-avoidant. People with this style of attachment experience a clashing fear of either being too close or too far away from their partners. People with this insecure attachment style have the characteristics of both the dismissive and preoccupied styles—their desire for closeness and their longing for connection are active, but because they have previous experiences of the ones they loved or depended on hurting them, they tend to feel uncomfortable relying on others or are even paralyzed by the fear that speaking their feelings and needs could be dangerous and make things worse. They might request attention from a partner but then withdraw when connection is offered or, in more extreme manifestations, they might demand attention or affection and then attack or criticize their partner when what they want is given. People with this style are easily overwhelmed by their feelings or subject to what I call *emotional flare-ups,* where their intense emotional states can take over, disrupting their ability to function and, at times, taking others down with them.

Due to their history of trauma, their sense of self and others have been impaired. When trauma occurs, there is a rupture with the foundational relationship a person has with their self. This severed internal relationship with the self needs to be restored so that the person can go on to trust and value themselves, as well as begin to trust others again. When this type of healing has yet to occur, people functioning from the fearful-avoidant attachment style will tend to see themselves as broken and unworthy and will expect that others are untrustworthy or will only hurt them in the end. In more extreme cases, this attachment style is associated with high relationship turmoil, dissatisfaction and toxicity, self-destructive behaviors, relationship abuse, mental illness and addictions.

Diane Poole Heller makes two important distinctions in regard to this attachment style. The first is that the expression of this style can either look more dismissive and withdrawing or more anxious, clingy and pursuing. Heller refers to these two variations as either being more *disorganized avoidant* or *disorganized anxious*. In my own practice, I make a distinction between the *internal fearful-avoidant* and the *external fearful-avoidant*. In the category of internal fearful-avoidant, we find people who, when under stress or threat, are triggered into higher anxiety and have the internal disorganized experience of wanting connection and wanting to move closer to someone, yet simultaneously feeling an inner pull back, believing the connection to be unsafe. However, such people do not act this dynamic out in ways that are destructive to themselves or others. The experience is more internally disruptive than externally damaging.

Other people express the experience of having one foot on the gas and the other on the brake in a relationship in a much more external and reactive way. These people react externally in ways that are confusing, contradictory or harmful. The distinction between internal and external fearful-avoidant might be a difference in degree or severity within this attachment style, or it might also be two different stages in healing. A person with a fearful-avoidant attachment style who has been engaging in healing work that is moving them towards more secure functioning may initially develop less external reactivity while still experiencing an inner "push/pull" dynamic. The process of resolving their trauma may have enabled them to now choose differently with how they externally respond.

The second important distinction that Heller makes is that we can have a *chronically* disorganized style that functions as a primary attachment style, or more of a *situational* disorganized style. In the situational kind, someone might be more consistently secure, dismissive or preoccupied in their attachment style, but in certain situations or under the influence of certain triggers, they get activated into a temporary disorganized state. Once the stressor or situation resolves, they then return to their other, more dominant style.

Since people with the fearful-avoidant style experience both attachment anxiety and attachment avoidance, see which of the above statements for the dismissive and preoccupied styles also describe your experience. Some statements that someone with a fearful-avoidant style might make are:

- I often don't feel safe or fully trusting in relationships, even if my partner acts in safe and trustworthy ways.
- I frequently get triggered by things that may seem to come out of nowhere.
- I genuinely want intimacy and closeness but I can experience episodes of fearful overwhelm when intimacy with a partner increases.
- When in conflict, I can vacillate from being overwhelmed or aggressive to being dismissive and numb.
- I can vacillate between different types of chaos or rigidity.
- When in distress I have acted in ways that have been harmful to myself or my partners.

- I often expect that the worst will happen in a relationship, even when things are going well.
- I have elaborate negative fantasies about what will go wrong or how my partner will inevitably hurt me beyond repair, even if things are mostly going well.
- Being in a relationship can cause me to become dysregulated, dissociative or confused.
- There are times when I look fine on the outside, but I am actually a complete tsunami on the inside.
- I frequently experience the conflicting internal drives of wanting to be close and share myself but fearing that closeness or vulnerability will be dangerous or cause the relationship to end.

Parental Interactions	Childhood Attachment Style	Adult Attachment Style
• Protective • Emotionally available • Responsive • Attuned	Secure	Secure 50–60%
• Unavailable • Unresponsive • Imperceptive or mis-attuned • Rejecting	Insecure: Avoidant	Dismissive 20–30%
• Inconsistently responsive, available or attuned • Intrusive • Acting out of their needs for attention or affection over the child's needs	Insecure: Anxious	Preoccupied 15–20%
• Frightening • Threatening • Frightened • Disorienting • Alarming	Insecure: Disorganized	Fearful-Avoidant 20–40%

TABLE 1.1: The types of parental interactions that are related to the different attachment styles in childhood, and how the names of the insecure styles change in adulthood. The percentages of each style are also noted. These percentages do not neatly add up to 100 percent since they are more of a general range, with each study finding slightly different percentages for each style (since people with a fearful-avoidant style might initially test as being one of the other insecure styles). Gender differences have not been found between the different styles.

An important takeaway from this overview of attachment theory is the importance of securely attaching to others who will care for us. This is our first survival strategy because without the loving and attentive presence from others we would die. Accordingly, emotional attunement and connection are wired into us as basic human needs that persist through life. Depending on the environment and circumstance that we were born into and how well our parents were able to meet our attachment needs (some conditions our parents had control of and others they did not) we will either develop a secure attachment style, where we feel safe to be with our caretakers and explore the world beyond them, or we will develop an insecure attachment style. Insecure attachment can take the form of overly pulling into ourselves to avoid and withdraw, overly turning outward to others to grasp and procure, or vacillating between the two. These insecure attachment styles are secondary survival strategies that make sense based on what we went through as a child and will continue to impact how we attach and bond in our adult romantic relationships. Here I invite you to reflect on your own personal attachment history, what style or styles you experienced with your different attachment figures and how this relates to the attachment behaviors you have exhibited in your adult romantic relationships.

CHAPTER TWO
THE DIFFERENT DIMENSIONS OF ATTACHMENT

MOST ATTACHMENT RESEARCHERS base their work on the idea of categorizing people under one of four specific types: secure, preoccupied, dismissive or fearful-avoidant. More recently, however, some researchers have proposed that attachment is better described using the two dimensions of attachment anxiety and attachment avoidance, and looking at the different ways these dimensions can interact.[29] They place each of these dimensions along an axis from high to low, and then cross the axes to form a diagram with four quadrants. While this model still produces the same four basic types (one per quadrant), it lets us see a few things in more nuanced ways based on how far along each axis we find ourselves. Not every person with a preoccupied attachment style is exactly the same, for instance. It also helps show the common ground between the different types; for example, both the fearful and the dismissive attachment styles share a higher level of emotional avoidance. This model can help us better understand how we might be able to move the needle on our own emotional tendencies when they're not serving us well.

Being high in the attachment anxiety dimension
relates to increased fears of being rejected, neglected,
abandoned or separated from an attachment figure. Being
low in attachment anxiety relates to being less fearful
or preoccupied that such things will occur. Attachment
avoidance is the dimension that relates to how comfortable or uncomfortable a person feels when it comes to
being close, intimate or reliant on a partner. Stated more
positively, low attachment avoidance refers to being more
comfortable with intimacy, closeness and reliance on a
partner and being more likely to approach and engage
with a partner.

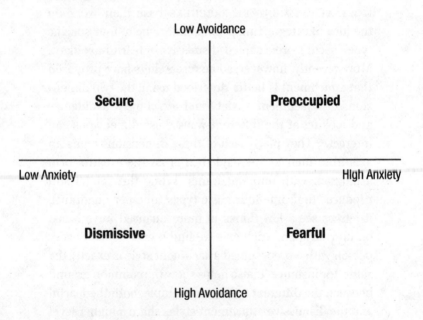

FIGURE 2.1: Attachment styles expressed using the two
dimensions of attachment anxiety and attachment avoidance.

The four different attachment styles relate to where people land on these two dimensions.

- When someone is low in attachment anxiety and low in attachment avoidance, they are in the secure attachment zone.
- When a person has low avoidance but high anxiety, their attachment style is preoccupied.
- Dismissive attachment happens when a person's anxiety is low, but their avoidance is high.
- When someone is high in both anxiety and avoidance, they have a fearful-avoidant style.

These dimensions also influence each other. For example, both the secure and preoccupied styles are low in attachment avoidance, but their differences in attachment anxiety will alter the way a person expresses their attachment. Someone lower in attachment anxiety will approach a partner from a more secure stance, moving towards them with a sense of openness, flexibility and interdependence, whereas someone who is higher in anxiety is more likely to seek proximity to their partner in order to grasp at or control them, be overly dependent on them, or simply to alleviate their own fears and anxiety.

On the flip side, the internal experience of being higher in attachment avoidance will be very different based on where someone is positioned on the attachment anxiety dimension. Someone who is high in avoidant behaviors but low in attachment anxiety might experience minimal internal conflict when there is increased distance from a partner—this person may not even recognize their own high avoidance. Someone who is equally high in avoidance but higher in anxiety can feel an enormous amount of internal conflict and distress. Their avoidance does not

necessarily feel like a safe refuge for them, but can feel
more like a freeze response. This person feels two things
at once: desire for proximity to a partner but fear of what
that closeness might bring.

I also think that the ways someone might experience being low in attachment anxiety will vary greatly
depending on where they lie in the attachment avoidance
dimension. For example, both the secure and dismissive
styles would be considered as being low in attachment
anxiety, but I don't think they are felt in the same way.
Someone who is more secure and lower in attachment
avoidance probably experiences little anxiety, whereas
for someone who is more dismissive and higher in
attachment avoidance, low anxiety is probably related to
the repressing or evading of anxious feelings rather than
not having them.

Both personally and professionally I have experienced
this four-quadrant model as more both more precise and
more useful than simply talking about the four attachment styles as stand-alone concepts. When I present
attachment in this way to workshop participants and
clients, they express being able to better place themselves
within these dimensions. We are then able to have much
more nuanced and empowering conversations about
approach/avoidance behaviors and low or high anxiety.
With this model, people seem better able to reflect on how
and why these dimensions play out (often differently) in
their relationships. Clients often describe feeling less
"pathologized" by this approach.

Speaking for myself, before learning about these
dimensions, I was often confused about exactly where I fit
within the three insecure styles. From going through the
Adult Attachment Interview (an interview and scoring

system developed to assess adult attachment) with my own therapist, I knew I had earned secure attachment, but there were still times when my insecure strategies arose, especially when under relational stress. I could place some of my behaviors in the dismissive style (I was self-reliant to a fault) but not all of them (I'm extremely empathic, comfortable with intimacy and emotionally focused). I could definitely relate to several of the ways the preoccupied style internally experiences things, but externally I was not presenting as the anxious preoccupied type at all. Some of my childhood experiences undoubtedly fall into the disorganized camp, but the initial descriptions of the fearful-avoidant style that I encountered were encumbered with much more volatility, toxicity and dysfunction than I had experienced in my adult life and relationships.

When I came across Mikulincer and Shaver's two-dimensional description of attachment I could immediately place myself as sometimes being high in anxiety and high in avoidance (fearful avoidance). Under certain circumstances, I experience internal anxiety, feel mentally preoccupied with relational dynamics and have emotional flare-ups in response to the slightest signal that a partner is withdrawing or low in their ability to be present and attuned. But externally, I was more likely to withdraw, play it cool and take the self-reliant route. My reaction could go unnoticed or be seen as me pulling in and withdrawing, but internally I was thrashing around, getting emotional whiplash from the "one foot on the gas and one foot on the brake" experience. The two-dimensional model offered more accuracy in understanding my own attachment style and helped me to identify the directions I still needed to focus on in my own healing.

I've found that many of my clients also describe relating to this style. They too are not presenting in the more extreme ways that the fearful-avoidant style is typically depicted, where mental illness, violence, abuse and/or forms of self-abuse are at play, but nonetheless they are functioning from this style and still need support in the unresolved trauma and pains that it surfaces from. These less extreme or overt expressions of fearful-avoidance can easily go undetected by professionals, leaving people confused about how to understand and identify their own attachment experiences. For any psychological model, there will always be people who do not neatly fit into what the theory or diagnostic criteria state, and when a typology is too rigid it can easily leave people to fall through the cracks. It is important that we recognize the significance of these different attachment categories and acknowledge that they are shining a beneficial light on specific patterns that arise for people. But we also need to hold these categorical descriptions with some flexibility. Different attachment patterns can exist on a spectrum, such as in this case with fearful-avoidant showing up in mild, moderate or more extreme expressions.

From Dysfunction to Desire

Another way to conceive of the attachment dimensions is not through their "dysfunctions," but through their strengths and desires. Defining the attachment styles through the dimensions of attachment avoidance and attachment anxiety can easily paint a bleak picture of dysfunction and leave people focusing on what's "wrong" with them. Based on this two-dimensional model, even a secure attachment, which is revered as the desired goal, is just being framed as how low in attachment anxiety and attachment avoidance it is, instead of being presented in its fullness with all the positive strengths and capacities that this attachment style embodies.

Let's take a person with a dismissive style as an example and look at how negative framing works. Because they're high on the avoidance axis and low on the anxiety axis, someone with a dismissive style is likely to use distancing and deactivating strategies when faced with relationship challenges. On the other end of the spectrum, someone in the preoccupied style sits low on the avoidance axis and high on the anxiety axis. Their strategies look more like hyperactivation and pursuing their partner in moments of relationship pain.

But we don't need to only use this negative framing of how these attachment-based emotional tendencies often play out. If instead of looking at how people with these insecure attachment styles jump to using either hyperactivating or deactivating strategies, we were to measure their levels of attachment avoidance or attachment anxiety, we can explore the positive aspects of these styles. Each of the different styles comes with its own strengths and values. The insecure attachment styles are not just survival strategies that kick into gear in response to attachment rupture or relationship distress. At their root, they can also be expressions of the essential human desires for autonomy and connection.

On one hand we have the need for agency, independence and choice, and on the other hand we have the need for closeness, connection, support and union. Ken Wilber, creator of integral theory, sees the horizontal dimension, the "anxiety" axis on the diagram above, as relating to drives that we all share. The basic human drive for agency sits on one end of the spectrum, and the equally human drive for communion sits at the other. All people, regardless of sex or gender, share these internal energies, capacities and drives for both autonomy and connection.

From this perspective, the dismissive style, which uses minimizing and dismissing strategies to dampen and cope with attachment distress, can also be seen as the strategy of someone who, when in less reactivity, is more aligned with their needs for autonomy and agency. In its healthier expression, people with a higher draw to autonomy can exhibit more highly developed abilities for self-sufficiency and competence in tending to the needs of the practical, logistical and material aspects of the world. They have the ability to compartmentalize emotions, which can be a very handy skill in certain circumstances. When these needs move too far outside of their healthy expressions, agency and autonomy can transform into feeling alienation and isolation, becoming emotionally unreachable, or refusing or even denying the need for connection or help from others. A person's boundaries can get too rigid, and they may shut others out and shut themselves too far in. When this happens, the values of autonomy and agency distort into more of a reactive strategy than a skillful expression of a person's needs.

Here's another example. The preoccupied style is based on hyperactivating strategies in response to attachment distress, and people with this style are often portrayed as being needy and codependent. But when someone is in the healthy range, this style can be reframed as being more aligned with the values of connection and togetherness. People with this style can have highly developed skills when it comes to identifying and attuning to the emotions of others, and they can be highly competent in tending to others' needs and handling the responsibilities of interpersonal relationships. When this goes too far, straying from its healthy expression, a person's communing drives can become unhealthy forms of enmeshment and fusion. They may lose themselves in a relationship and see a decreased ability to truly know themselves or even make up their own minds.

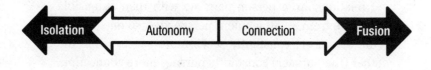

FIGURE 2.2: How the values and drives for agency and communion can go beyond their healthier manifestations and turn into either self-alienation or self-abandonment.

To navigate our relationships from a place of health and wholeness, we need to learn how to manage these seemingly contradictory drives. We need to find ways to feel sovereign without losing our connection to others, and to be in communion with others without losing our sense of self. The healthy range on this spectrum corresponds to the skills and abilities of the secure attachment style, where a person is able to embrace their autonomy without fear of abandonment, as well as dive deep into intimacy and connection without the concern of engulfment.

Attachment researcher Mary Main posits that, in childhood, secure attachment arises when a parent responds in a sensitive way to their child's need for both autonomous exploration and proximity and comfort.[30] The dismissive attachment style results from parents who discourage their child's proximity-seeking attachment behaviors, and the preoccupied attachment style develops from the experience of having parents who discourage autonomy. Being open and responsive to the full spectrum of our attachment needs is important for embodying the fullness of our emotional capacities as adults.

A common predicament that arises in relationships is referred to as the distancer-pursuer dance. In this type of relationship, a person pairs up with their ostensible opposite from an attachment perspective, so one partner (the distancer) constantly seeks more space, while the other (the pursuer) constantly pursues more connection. As the distancer attempts to take physical or emotional space, the pursuer moves in closer to try to bridge the gap. The closer that the pursuer comes, the more the distancer pulls back, which then provokes the pursuer to move in even more. The pursuer never catches up, while the distancer never fully gets the breathing room they need. The pursuer fears that they will be abandoned, while the distancer fears being engulfed.

In this dance, both partners are left frustrated and unable to get their needs met, often missing that this archetypal pattern has more to do with their inner self than their partner, who is just serving as a mirror reflecting back the parts of them that have been exiled and disowned. The distancer has cast off the parts of their self that yearn for closeness and connection and that desperately fear being abandoned. They are drawn to the pursuer, who will act these needs and fears out for them so that the distancer doesn't have to. The pursuer, in turn, has projected outward the parts of their self that crave autonomy and independence and that are actually afraid of truly being vulnerable, being seen and being close. The pursuer is drawn to the distancer, who will act out these needs and fears for them so that they don't have to. They are both trying to achieve wholeness, which is what keeps them dancing, but it's the dance itself that prevents them from taking responsibility for the parts of themselves they have disowned; they instead blame their partners for enacting these elements of themselves.

When I began working with these aspects of autonomy and connection within myself, I came across the dilemma of how to bring these two poles together. Initially, when I conceived of these drives as existing on a spectrum, they often felt in opposition to each other, with only one need or drive being attainable at a time, usually at the expense of the other. How could I inch myself more towards communion without compromising my integrity, and how could I move more towards my independence without compromising my connections? So, when in doubt, I've learned it can be useful to switch metaphors. Instead of seeing these needs and attachment expressions as existing on a continuum, a two-dimensional space in which you can only occupy one position at a time, what if we conceive of the needs for autonomy and connection as the two reins of secure functioning? When riding a horse, we use two reins to control and direct the horse. If we want to turn left, we tighten our grip to tug on the left rein, simultaneously loosening the other rein. We do the opposite to move right. The terrain ahead is constantly changing, and so the reins in our hands are constantly readjusting. With time and practice, we gain the ability to simultaneously tighten and loosen the reins without tightening so hard that we hurt or jerk the horse, or loosening so much so that communication and direction are lost.

To best respond to whatever arises in front of us day by day or even moment by moment, we sometimes need to tighten up on the reins of autonomy, while loosening the reins of connection. In other moments, we tighten the connection reins, moving in closer to our partners while releasing the autonomy reins. In her book *Mating in Captivity*, Esther Perel warns us how too much closeness can collapse into fusion and that too much distance impedes connection. She advises that we need both separateness and connection for intimacy and eroticism, so when it comes to secure functioning, I would say that we must be able to "straddle" both of these needs simultaneously. With practice, we learn that autonomy and connection aren't an either/or experience but a both/and experience. We can be both different and connected. With practice we can also learn how to ebb and flow between the two states with more skill and grace, using both reins simultaneously to embrace both our independence and our dependency, our autonomy and our connection.

Boundaries and the Giving and Receiving of Love

Our boundaries are the ways we protect ourselves physically, mentally and emotionally. They are how we establish our sovereignty, as well as how we open ourselves to others. Our boundaries are the meeting point between ourselves and another—the point at which we can be both separate and connected. Our boundaries guide us in navigating our relationships and they are directly related to the ways in which we are able to give and receive love. When we've experienced attachment wounds as children or adults, we can experience disruptions in our ability to give love, receive love, or both. If connection and love from our care-takers was absent, inconsistent or dangerous, we may want love from others, but then have difficulty fully letting it in. We can struggle to believe that it is safe and real, that it doesn't have strings attached, and that it's here to stay (or at least that it won't immediately leave). It can be extremely vulnerable to try to let people into the deeper places and we may not even allow ourselves to go there. Soaking up the love from our partners and allowing it to penetrate into our bones and cells can be foreign and frightening.

Giving love can also feel problematic when we have attachment wounds. We are unsure whether our partners will receive it, see it as enough, reject it, take it for granted or take advantage of it. We might wonder whether our love will be reciprocated or if we will we be left standing on the relational edge alone? Giving love can be just as vulnerable as receiving it because when we give, we are taking the risk of revealing our hearts. We're declaring our desire to be close to someone and we are potentially exposing our limitations in the process.

When we have attachment insecurity we may find ourselves struggling on both the giving and receiving ends. We may either over-take or under-take from others, as well as over-give or under-give to our partners. All these are forms of boundary issues.

In the book *Loving Bravely*, Alexandra H. Solomon defines healthy boundaries as the balancing point where you are able to both connect to another as well as be separate from another, maintaining your own energy and sense of self while your partner maintains the energy that is theirs. Similar to how we need both autonomy and connection to be in secure functioning, we need to have *connection* and *protection* in concert with each other to maintain healthy boundaries. Our boundaries begin to become unhealthy when we're either underprotected or overprotected towards others, as well as when we're being too connected or not connected enough. Solomon further describes boundaries as either being too porous or too rigid in terms of what we allow in from others and how we give outwardly to others. Porous boundaries arise when we are connected but not protected, and rigid boundaries stem from being protected, but not connected.

	Input	Output
Healthy Boundaries Being connected and protected.	We can connect with others, while also maintaining our sense of self. We can take in love from others.	We share our feelings, opinions and perspectives, while respecting and allowing others to be distinct and separate from us. We can give to others.
Porous Boundaries Being connected but not protected.	Over-receiving: We absorb and allow in what is not ours. We lose our sense of self.	Over-giving: We intrude onto others, inserting our thoughts, feelings, opinions, perspectives or sense of self into them.
Rigid Boundaries Being protected but not connected.	Under-receiving: We block out the input and love of others.	Under-giving: We restrain ourselves from expressing or giving to others.

TABLE 2.1: Healthy, porous and rigid boundaries, adapted from *Loving Bravely* by Alexandra H. Solomon.

Porous Boundaries

According to Solomon, when our boundaries are porous on the input, we are *absorbing,* and when they are too porous on the output we are *intruding*. When our boundaries are porous from the outside in, we are being too wide open. We let other people's thoughts, opinions, preferences and judgments eclipse our own inclinations, wisdom or better knowledge. Absorbing is when we take in what is not ours, when we lack enough self-definition that we leave ourselves underprotected while being over-connected. When our boundaries are porous from the inside out, we become intrusive to others, trying to inhabit their skin or meddling too much in their business. We are intruding when we give unsought advice or tell people what they should or shouldn't do in the name of helping them. Usually the help we're offering was either unsolicited or not a match to what the other person actually needs. Intruding also includes crossing or ignoring other people's boundaries, especially when those lines have been articulated. In both cases of porous boundaries, we may find ourselves feeling overly responsible for others, either absorbing or intruding in order to fix, accommodate, people please or overcompensate.

Rigid Boundaries

Rigid boundaries are a sign that we are overfocused on protection without allowing sufficient connection. When our boundaries are rigid on the input, we are *blocking* and when they are too rigid on the output we are *restraining*. When our boundaries are rigid from the inside out we are obstructing input from others, whether that is their love, attention, feedback or requests. When blocking, we are guarding what comes in and disallowing the influence of others, usually from fear of being hurt or attacked. When blocking, we can come off as prickly, abrupt, edgy, defensive, frozen or withdrawn. When our boundaries are rigid from the inside out we restrain ourselves from expressing what is true for us internally. We restrain our feelings (positive or negative), thoughts, preferences, requests and even the affection we have for others. Restraining is usually the result of feeling unsafe in expressing ourselves, so we instead hold back and hold in to try to stay protected at the expense of being connected. In either version of rigid boundaries, we are holding tight to our emotional armor, restricting the flow of love and expression coming in or out.

Questions to Consider

- How do you find yourself over-giving in relationships? What beliefs about yourself play into this? What beliefs about others play into this?
- How do you find yourself under-giving in relationships? What beliefs about yourself play into this? What beliefs about others play into this?
- In what ways do you find yourself over-receiving or over-taking in relationships? What beliefs about yourself or about others play into this?
- In what ways do you find yourself under-receiving in relationships? What beliefs about yourself or about others play into this?
- In what ways do you experience your boundaries as porous, whether by being absorbing, being intrusive or both?
- In what ways do you experience your boundaries as rigid, whether by blocking, restraining or both?

- Do you need to focus more on tightening up your boundaries and protection of yourself, whether on the input or output? How can you do this?
- Do you need to focus more on softening the rigidity of your boundaries and allowing more connection, whether on the input or output? How can you do this?

CHAPTER THREE
THE NESTED MODEL OF ATTACHMENT AND TRAUMA

SO FAR, WE HAVE COVERED the different attachment styles and looked at how these relate to the different dimensions of attachment avoidance and attachment anxiety, as well as the horizontal dimension of autonomy and connection. In this next chapter I offer an additional perspective to our discussion of attachment in an attempt to diversify the levels or dimensions at which we consider and contemplate our attachment experiences. This will support our discussion of attachment and nonmonogamy in Part Two. It is difficult to talk about attachment without talking about trauma and so before I present on these different levels, a definition of trauma is also needed.

The word trauma comes from the Greek word "wound," which was initially used to refer to physical injuries. The definition has since expanded to further encompass psychological and spiritual wounds as well. In many ways, the lasting psychological impact of trauma has become much more central to the study and treatment of trauma than the physical, since mental and emotional symptoms can persist long after the physical body has healed and many traumas occur without the body even being touched.

Trauma can result from a single event, a series of events or multiple sets of circumstances that cause physical, emotional, psychological or spiritual harm. Single-incident traumas include one-off events such as robberies, assaults, accidents or natural disasters. Complex and relational trauma are terms used to describe the experience of multiple traumatic events that are ongoing, such as abuse or neglect, and that are interpersonal in nature. Traumatic events and experiences can be especially impactful in the earlier years of life. A distressing event at a young age can potentially negatively impact brain development, and if it is perpetrated by an attachment figure, it can be particularly harmful. Our fundamental sense of self and sense of safety in the world can be painfully called into question when the ones we are dependent on either can't keep us safe or are the ones we need protection from.

Traumas are the events and situations that overwhelm us, leaving us feeling out of control, helpless and alone. Not everyone experiences trauma the same way, and not everyone who goes through the same events will necessarily be traumatized. Trauma occurs on a continuum of stress, and the difference between a traumatic experience versus a bad or stressful experience is the impact on our body's ability to recover. When something stressful occurs, our bodies are wired to release an entire cocktail of chemicals into our bloodstream to activate the sympathetic nervous system's fight/flight/freeze/appease defense response. This is meant to be a short-term strategy to keep us alive. Once the event is over, our bodies are supposed to return to a state of parasympathetic nervous system balance, where we can function as usual in a calm and clear-minded way. But bigger traumatic events can activate our natural stress response to such a degree that our nervous system is overwhelmed and dysregulated to the point that this chemical cocktail is unable to be processed and we are left unable to fully recover. This can have a lasting effect on the nervous system, and when left untreated, trauma can interfere with our ability to inhabit our bodies, exhibit mental flexibility, function in everyday ways, learn, grow, love and securely attach. Left unresolved, trauma can cause us to experience ongoing adverse effects on our physical, psychological, social, occupational and spiritual well-being.

However, enormous stressors or big overwhelming events are not the only ways that a person's nervous system can be activated and overwhelmed to the point of experiencing trauma. We can also experience smaller but ongoing stressful events that have a cumulative harmful effect. Instead of getting a single massive blast of the survival cocktail into our bloodstream when we experience a car accident, a natural disaster or a physical assault, we can get little blasts throughout the day from experiences like demanding work environments, relationship tension, health issues, life transitions, traffic jams, parenting, etc. Our bodies need time to metabolize the chemical cocktail released from stress and when we are in a chronic state of stress—whether big or small, physical, emotional, psychological, environmental or existential—we can get pushed over the edge into a state of sympathetic nervous system dominance. This means that the survival response that was meant to be temporary has now become constant. The threat that we experience does not even need to be real, but the repeated perception of a threat, day after day, can push our nervous system into a traumatized state. When this happens, we are living in survival mode, stuck is sympathetic dominance and unable to access our ability to recover and thrive.

Some trauma experts have begun to further simplify the definition of trauma, framing it as the experience of broken connection. From an attachment perspective this makes sense, since broken connection with an attachment figure could mean death to an infant or young child and so being disconnected from our attachment figures can be in and of itself traumatic. But the trauma of broken connection also occurs through the massive disconnection that someone has with their self and another when enacting interpersonal harm.

Attachment is related to this, since having a history of secure attachment acts as a protective buffer against trauma. Research shows that in the aftermath of trauma, people who are well-connected with others are more likely to recover faster and less likely to experience post-traumatic stress disorder (PTSD). Conversely, people with a disorganized attachment history are more likely to develop PTSD after traumatic experiences. Seeing trauma as a result of broken connection also makes it difficult to tease trauma and attachment apart from each other, since the absence of safe nurturing relationships can lead to trauma, and having safe and nurturing relationships can serve as a shield in the face of other traumas. As you will see in the nested model of attachment and trauma, trauma and attachment wounds are not just an individual or relational experience. They also stem from the world we are in, where injustice and power imbalances still exist, and where generations of cultural and collective

traumas have been unaddressed, all shaping and informing our experiences.

The Nested Model of Attachment and Trauma

Attachment unfolds over multiple levels of the human
experience. When referring to different levels of experience, I am pointing to the different dimensions or aspects
of our human experience: self, relationships, home, local
communities and culture, societal, and the global or collective. These different levels may seem separate and different from one another, yet they are all interconnected,
with each level acting as an important ingredient to our
experience and informing any given moment, as well as
the decisions we make.

To offer a simple example, if I am looking to buy a new
car, there are several different facets or levels of my life
that can influence my decision. At the self level, I might
think about which car most appeals to me based on my
individual preferences, likes, dislikes, needs and what I
can afford. If I expand beyond my personal perspective to
the relational level, I will consider which car would be best
for my family, including my son's needs. Additionally, the
cultural level informs what kind of car I would consider
purchasing based on how I do or do not want to be perceived by others. The range of cars I have access to in the
US falls under the societal level, and considerations such
as electric versus gas come under the global or collective
level. In discussion of the nested model of attachment and
trauma, I will refer to the different facets, dimensions or
perspectives of our lives that coalesce into the whole of
our experience, even if we're unaware of them.

The current literature on attachment predominantly focuses on the self and relationship levels. That is, on identifying our individual attachment styles and considering them in connection to our relationship experiences. Concentrating on just these two levels of experience is perfectly understandable since our relational level experiences of having our attachment needs met or not shape how the self is formed and developed. Subsequently, the attachment style that arises at the self level feeds back into the relational level, informing how we show up within our relationships. In many ways, we can see attachment as a nice feedback loop in which relationships shape the individual and individuals then shape their relationships, with relationships further re-shaping the individual and so on repeatedly.

We could easily keep the discussion limited to these two levels, but there are additional facets to our experience of attachment and trauma that are important to explore. The levels of home, culture, society and the collective all factor into how safe and secure we feel in the world, with others and within ourselves. If we fail to include these levels in our understanding of attachment and trauma, we run the risk of either reducing experiences that impact attachment to the self or relationship levels when they are actually occurring at *another* level, or we run the risk of missing these factors altogether. For example, consider poverty, gender expectations or institutionalized birth practices, and how each of these may impact attachment and trauma. Since all of the levels of experience are not actually separate from one another—each level interacts with and influences the others—I have chosen to present them as nested.

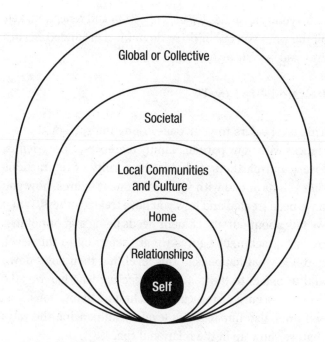

FIGURE 3.1: The nested model of attachment and trauma.

Self Level

The innermost circle represents you: the individual self who has a certain temperament, a one-of-a-kind genetic and epigenetic expression, a specific attachment history and a unique way of experiencing those attachment styles. This circle holds the interior experience of your thoughts and feelings, how you see and identify yourself and how you perceive, interpret and think about others. Here reside all of your skills and abilities, as well as your longings, aversions, hopes and fears. All of the ways that you do or do not take care of yourself reside in this circle, as do your capacities for introspection and reflection, and all the ways you either do or do not feel grounded, secure and safe in your own being.

Relationship Level

This level refers to your one-on-one interpersonal experiences with your parents, family members, close friends, lovers and partners. It holds the quality of interactions that you have had with your attachment figures, how you have been treated and how you have treated others. When we talk about our attachment needs being met or not met by our attachment figures we are referring to this level, and it is what happens at this level that then flows down and transfers to the self level, affecting whether we take on more secure or insecure attachment adaptations. The self level also impacts this level by influencing the ways that we show up in the relational space.

At this level, traumatic experiences such as physical, sexual or emotional abuse, neglect or intimate partner violence all play a part in our ability to attach. Complex and relational trauma can occur from ongoing harm or abandonment from a primary attachment figure—whether from a parent or from a romantic partner as an adult. When mistreatment and harm occur from a trusted loved one, the effect can be especially damaging to the attachment system, bringing into question whether anyone is safe to be trusted and relied on. Single-incident traumas such as car accidents, medical procedures or a one-time assault may not have originated from this relational level, but they will also impact a person's ability to securely attach at this level. Regardless of which level our attachment wounds first take place in, our insecure attachment styles can be healed through this relationship level. This can occur by having our needs met from attuned responsive partners or even having reparative experiences with the ones we have been hurt by.

Research and literature on attachment have provided undeniable evidence about how relationships with our parents and lovers shape our attachment style, but the impact of siblings is not as commonly discussed, despite being just as important to our attachment style. In therapy, I've seen many clients who identify their interactions with siblings as the source of their attachment wounds. Sometimes this stems from parents who neglect to protect siblings from each other—placing one sibling's needs over the other's or practicing outright favoritism—but other times the disruption is directly between the siblings. Attachment ruptures with siblings can occur when there has been overt emotional or verbal abuse, bullying, physical abuse or outright rejection. Disconnection resulting from a large age or personality difference, competitiveness and consistent mis-attuned teasing also show up in the therapy room as attachment disruptions from sibling relationships. These experiences can impact a person's ability to make meaningful connections with romantic partners as an adult.

Culturally, in the West, we tend to see romantic and parental relationships as superior in influence to others, and studies have shown that adult attachments are mostly directed towards a romantic/sexual partner over adult friendships.[31] But our relationships with siblings or close friends can function as some of the most important attachment bonds that we have. For many, a friend or sibling can serve as a primary attachment figure, and when there has been attachment wounding with partners or parents, it is these very connections that can provide the corrective attachment experiences and healing from the attachment disruptions we've had with others at the relational level. Friendships that function as a primary attachment can also leave a painful mark on one's heart and a significant attachment disturbance when there is betrayal, dishonesty, ghosting or drama that ends in the loss of the friendship. Death or loss of a close friend can create massive shock waves in our attachment systems.

Home Level

This next level goes beyond the one-to-one interactions at the relational level and considers the ways in which our family interacted as a whole and how our actual physical home impacted our attachment. This includes the number of people in your home, the type of home culture and place you grew up in, how many generations of family were living in your home, whether you had to go back and forth between your parents' homes due to separation or divorce and whether or not you even had a home. These factors can all have a supportive or straining influence on your ability to attach and feel safe with the people you live with.

Were you one of eight siblings and felt like there was an abundance of love and attention? Did you always have someone to talk to or play with? Or were you one of eight siblings who competed for food or attention, and your needs easily got lost in the crowd? Were there multiple generations in your home, which might have filled the gaps or created a bridge between you and your parents, or did having a multigenerational home detract from what your parents were able to offer you? Were there sick people in your house? Did you have a blended home with stepparents and stepsiblings? Were you an introvert (self level) living within a family of extroverts, or an artist living with a family of scientists? Were there pets in your home that you bonded with, or pets that you were allergic to? What habits and routines did your family have, and how did they impact your attachment experience? All of these experiences at the home level can influence our sense of belonging and whether or not we feel safe and secure within ourselves, our relationships and in the world.

This level also includes the physical environment, such as whether or not you *liked* your childhood physical home and bedroom (if you had one) and felt safe there. If the home was too messy or too clean, too quiet or too noisy, or otherwise not well-matched with you, it could potentially create stress and tension in the nervous system, prodding us into survival stress responses. One therapy client of mine was able to connect how her current preoccupied attachment style was related to her experience of moving homes too many times as a child. Her relational-level experience of attachment with her parents was very secure, but moving homes four times in just a few short years created a sense of constant underlying uneasiness in her body due to the repeated loss of friends, school and home. She developed a mental storyline that whenever she got comfortable and started to feel settled in a new place, the rug got ripped from right under her. Consistency of home was very important to her and this uneasiness created from the home level was now impacting her ability to trust that her romantic partner's affection could be stable and enduring at the relational level, causing her to experience higher levels of attachment anxiety.

Another client reflected on how their experience of living in a rat-infested home contributed to their higher levels of attachment avoidance. Living among rats meant that there were certain closets, drawers, even rooms in their home that they steered clear of to avoid a rat encounter. The only way they felt safe was to withdraw into the few locations in their apartment that were relatively rat-free. In therapy, they came to see how this withdrawal included the minimizing of their desire for connection with their parents and siblings because wanting to be close to others would have required them to go into parts of the house that felt unsafe. As they got older and more social, they felt too embarrassed to have friends over and would often spend more time at friends' homes to avoid their own. The shame and embarrassment that they experienced at the self level because of their home-level environment contributed to higher levels of attachment avoidance and discomfort with intimacy at the relational level. As this client and I processed through their early attachment experiences at the home level and restored a sense of safety in their nervous system around what it felt like to be in their home now, they were then able to shift into more secure functioning at the self and relationship levels.

Local Culture and Communities Level

Sometimes, stressors, traumas and attachment struggles come from beyond the home, relational or self levels, and instead stem from the culture and communities that we are embedded in. The local culture and community level refers to the places where we spend our time outside of our home, such as work, school, friends' houses, the gym and clubs, as well as sports venues and religious or spiritual centers. Culture can be rich, complex and contrasting, and we may find ourselves within several different cultures and communities that each have a different set of social rules, ways of relating and expectations for what it means to be an accepted member. People who do not fit into the norms of their communities can experience attachment insecurity and trauma if they feel that being themselves or expressing who they are will cause harm or be danger-ous. If we have to conceal and contort who we are, our foundational relationship with our self can get severed and interfere with how we then experience the levels of relationship and home. Unfortunately, many people expe-rience harm or violation by trusted community members, mentors, teachers or clergy. These experiences can leave a lasting mark on how safe someone feels in groups, as well as how worthy someone feels about being able to give and receive love.

Growing up in Brooklyn, New York, I was fortunate to be invited into the homes of my friends, many of whom were first-generation Americans. The ways my friend's Cuban mother spoke to, disciplined, cared for and touched her child were vastly different from the ways my Irish American friends were treated by their parents, which were both considerably distinct from the Italian, Russian, Puerto Rican, African American and Greek homes I entered. Some families were affectionate and effusive, others were distant and stoic. Some were phys-ically present and practically consistent, but emotionally hesitant. Looking back, I can see how the ways that each of my friends was parented had a lot to do with the language, culture and religion of their parents, with each culture having different expectations about what it meant to be a parent, what discipline was, how and when you used it, and how a child was supposed to behave. These cultural narratives, which are often implicit and taken for granted, shaped how available, responsive and attuned these parents were to their children's attachment needs.

Today, the local culture and communities level also includes virtual culture and online communities. We can physically be in our homes but have our minds and hearts somewhere else completely, in the virtual world. In their online course *Secure Attachment Parenting in the Digital Age*, Diane Poole Heller and Kim John Payne discuss the particular challenges that our current society faces regarding attachment and technology. They highlight the potentially damaging effects that overuse of technology has on both the parent and child's ability to develop emotional bonds. The addition of screens into our already busy lives can add further strain on important face-to-face connection time between parents and their children.

While use of technology is more and more of a social requirement at even very young ages, for many parents it is also a needed crutch, often due to financial necessity. If all the adults in the home need to work, screen time can become the babysitter or give the parents the break that they need just to make dinner or maintain the bare basics of their home. Even though we are ostensibly more connected than ever through our phones, tablets and other devices, studies have shown[32] that, in adults in the US aged 19 to 32, higher social media use can lead to feeling more socially isolated and emotionally disconnected than people with lower social media use. I also see how emotionally overwhelming it can be when the absence of face-to-face contact enables a certain boldness or even meanness from people that they would not necessarily enact in person. Online attacks and rejections of others can cause a great deal of loss and psychological injury. As in all levels, there can be damage and trauma at the local culture and communities level, but there can, of course, also be healing. When someone grows up in a home or town where no one really looks and feels like they do, finding an online community where their voice and experiences are received, honored and even celebrated can be deeply healing to their sense of self and connection.

School culture is another important aspect to this level, since most children spend the majority of their waking hours in the classroom, cafeterias and school-yard. I once had a client who joked that you should never trust anyone who said they liked their junior high school experience. I later learned that this comment was the sarcastic mask in front of some very painful and trau-matic events she experienced in early adolescence. Now in her 40s, this woman had lasting scars from the social hierarchies and mean girl culture at her junior high school. She had experienced overt social rejection and repeated emotional and verbal cruelty from her peers. Coupled with the highly competitive academic culture of her school, the educational and social pressures became too unbearable and thus she attempted to take her life at age 13.

While I was writing this book, my father sent me a newspaper article in which he was interviewed about the sexual assault he experienced from his high school principal over 40 years earlier. In the article, he is quoted as relating the alcoholism, drug addiction and mental illness of his adult life as having its origin in the profound shame he experienced from being sexually assaulted at school. When I spoke to him about it, he also added that the years of corporal punishment and the Catholic school culture of overt disapproval further reinforced and solidified his shame. His traumas at this level had a lasting effect on his ability to bond with me as my parent. When I was eight years old, my father went into rehab, but his sobriety did not initially improve our relationship as much as both of us might have anticipated. Although the alcoholism and drug addiction were treated, his trauma, shame and deep-rooted feeling of unworthiness to be loved—even from his own child—remained for decades. My father had a strong desire to be available to me, but the absence of healing from his high school traumas and the ensuing shame left him, in many ways, incapable of bonding, connecting and responding in the nurturing, present and attuned ways that both of us wanted.

How safe we feel on the streets of our neighborhood, whether we have to lock our front door or not, how welcome and embraced we feel from the communities that we encounter and whether the leaders of our various communities are benevolent or unkind are all factors that I see as impacting our sense of safety, security and ability to explore. Traumas that arise from bullying, community violence or school shootings should not be underestimated. But although many different types of attachment traumas can happen at this level, it is also a level that can offer needed healing and attachment repair. The homes of friends, spiritual communities, substance abuse support groups, sports and dance teams or online communities can become our safe havens where we are freer to be ourselves, are understood and are seen and loved for who we are.

Social Level

The next outer dimension in this nested model refers to the larger societal structures and systems that we live in, such as our economic, legal, medical and political systems, as well as our religious institutions. It is at the social level that prejudice and oppression are institutionalized through the laws and power structures that either favor or discriminate against people based on age, race, sex, class, physical ability, sexual orientation and relationship orientation (including monogamy and polyamory). Who is considered legally legitimate or not at a societal level, who has access to health care and education, whether or not you have rights to your children or whether or not you are subject to the institutionalization of birth practices that can interfere with parent-child bonding are all factors that can be traumatizing and attachment-compromising. Additionally, whether or not we are a part of a legally protected class has massive implications for how safe and secure we feel in the world. The sociologist Johan Galtung refers to this as *structural violence*.[33] Distinguished from physical violence (yet often intertwined), structural violence refers to a type of violence that is often invisible yet intricately built into social structures. People's lives are complicated, confined or even lost because of heterosexism, classism, racism, ableism and sexism. Structural violence may be less obvious and direct than physical violence, but it is just as impactful and harmful. It creates a disparity between a person's potential reality—the life they could conceivably live—compared to the limited reality that they find themselves in.

Societal issues including homophobia, racism, sexism and mononormativity do not exist solely at the societal

level. They influence and play out in very real and impactful ways, including the neighborhoods and homes we live
in, which schools we have access to and what funding they
receive, how we approach or avoid others and how we are
treated by teachers, taxi drivers or clerks at the grocery
store. A black man is likely to have a very different experience of how safe and secure he feels when walking past
a police officer than a white woman in the same scenario.
In a time when mass shootings are rampant in the US and
amid the current political climate, a person of color who
practices Islam will likely feel very differently walking
into a mosque than a white Catholic person walking into
a church. These societal experiences can then trickle all
the way down to the self level, where social-level issues
become internalized as forms of shame or self-loathing,
again hindering one's ability to bond, attach and connect.
Studies have shown that children with socioeconomic
risks are more likely to develop disorganized attachment[34]
and that children are at an increased risk of disorganized
attachment when they are in non-maternal care for more
than 60 hours a week, due to parental work hours.[35]

Is it honestly possible to feel safe and secure in a
capitalist society that defines our human value based on
what we do and how much we make, rather than who we
are? Is it honestly possible to feel safe and secure in a
society that bombards us with messages asserting (even
aggressing) that in order to be secure in our self or with
our place in the world we need to acquire more money,
more religion, more objects, more products, more body-
altering procedures or more property? Society teaches
us how to love and who is worthy of love via the media,
commercials and through institutionalized practices such
as tax benefits for married couples. Relationships are

defined as valuable and potential partners are evaluated as worthy based on how much money is spent on dinner, date nights, vacations, diamonds and wedding arrangements. Flipping to the other extreme and thinking that money doesn't matter or is unimportant in a relationship can also be damaging, since we live in a society where money is a basic requirement for survival. It's difficult to show up and thrive in relationships when we can't feed ourselves, pay the bills or afford basic health care.

In addition to the ways that capitalism can influence who and how we love, in couples therapy I regularly witness how patriarchal values and gender discourses eclipse intimate connection and attachment. Developing healthy relational attachment requires feelings of safety and security. While significant achievements have been made for women over the past several decades, many women still experience sexism, objectification, invisibility, exclusion or even servitude within their most intimate relationships. My generation was taught that girls can do anything that boys can do, but most of my peers still feel the need to have to shave, pluck, color, tint, laser, push up or add extensions to parts of their bodies just to achieve baseline attractiveness and feel good enough to walk out the door every day.

For many women, feminism has added more criteria to what it means to be a woman. In commenting on how increased racial and ethnic diversity in Hollywood has had a positive change on body image, the comedian Tina Fey credits women like Jennifer Lopez and Beyoncé for revising the definition of American beauty. Being skinny is no longer the only ideal, but having a larger butt and thighs is now also considered desirable. These changes have definitely added more nuance to our beauty standards and represent positive developments, particularly for racialized women, larger-bodied women, trans women and disabled women who have typically been found wanting or lesser-than in comparison to the narrow beauty norms of privileged thin, cisgender, able-bodied white women. However, Tina Fey points out, these changes did not necessarily emancipate all women to embrace their body as it is, but rather,

> ... added to the laundry list of attributes women must have to qualify as beautiful. Now every girl is expected to have: Caucasian blue eyes, full Spanish lips, a classic button nose, hairless Asian skin with a California tan, a Jamaican dance hall ass, long Swedish legs, small Japanese feet, the abs of a lesbian gym owner, the hips of a nine-year-old boy, the arms of Michelle Obama and doll tits.[36]

In addition to inflated beauty standards, women are now also expected to be career-driven, achievement-orientated, financially independent, and a competent badass in the boardroom, bedroom, kitchen and nursery.

On the flip side, the plights of men are often dismissed and unseen, since men are regarded as the ones wielding all the privilege and power. But what happens when the same societal structures that grant men superiority also deny them the full range of human emotions and threaten their status as men if they experience even the slightest form of sensitivity, vulnerability or indication of their needs for love, emotional safety and tenderness (basically, if men admit to having any attachment needs at all)? What happens when men are paralyzed by shame and made to feel unworthy of love and partnership unless they meet certain masculine expectations around financial or professional success? And what happens to a person's ability to feel safe and connected when they are transgender or do not fit in the gender binary at all? Many of the personal problems and relationship struggles that we face are actually societal issues impairing our ability to bond, connect and love in secure ways.

Global or Collective Level

The earth is alive. It is where we come from, it is what nourishes life and it is where we will return to. If we are going to talk about attachment relationships it would be remiss not to mention our original mother: Mother Earth. For many of us, our relationship to the environment is dissociative and overly abstracted. Even though the earth is the very ground upon which we move, we still see it as separate, unaffected and removed from our daily existence. Growing up in New York City, it was frequently modeled to me that the ground was not a place to revere or enjoy. This was mostly because actual areas of earth and grass in the city were few and far between. What I saw instead was that the earth was something to pour concrete over, to drive over, to blast through, to take for granted or the place to literally throw your trash. The earth was more of a means to an end, a resource to take from instead of a living entity to be in relationship with. I think it's safe to say that in the US, many people have a dismissive attachment to the earth. They downplay its importance, cutting off any potential experience of wisdom or intimacy that could be gained through connection with the natural world.

On a daily basis, people are immediately confronted with the sudden and overwhelming realities of our planet through fires, floods, hurricanes, earthquakes, tornados, tsunamis, volcanoes and pandemics. Needless to say, it can be traumatizing to lose loved ones, homes, and entire communities in natural disasters. Access to post-disaster aid and support can also be further traumatizing when poverty, racism or public policy further influence who, how and when people are helped. In a 2019 TED Talk, *How Climate Change Affects Your Mental Health*, Britt Wray articulates the ways in which natural disasters can lead to increased PTSD and suicide in survivors. She addresses how our changing environment threatens our social, mental, relational and spiritual health, and how some psychologists are treating "pre-traumatic stress" in regard to climate change.[37] Zhiwa Woodbury explains that humans are being confronted with a new type of trauma that has never been confronted before—one that is ongoing and continuous without immediate solutions, and which calls into question our shared identity as humans. In an article titled "Climate Trauma: Towards a New Taxonomy of Traumatology," he writes:

> *Climate Trauma is an* ever-present existential threat *with a bevy of constant cognitive remind-ers—melting ice caps; eroding shorelines; waves of homeless refugees; the ravaging storms, floods, and fires broadcast into our homes 24/7; and the constant roll-call of disappearing species, vanishing rain forests, and dying coral reefs. There are certain things in life that we cannot "unsee," and Climate Trauma indelibly stamps our*

> *consciousness in that way, fundamentally altering*
> *the way we see the world and our place in it.*[38]

Not everyone is currently or directly in harm's way of natural disasters, but many of us still experience climate trauma or a preoccupied attachment to the earth by living in daily anxiety about the state of our water, air pollution, the state of forests, the loss of biodiversity and the extinction of animal species, just to name a few.

For one of my clients, the bulk of our therapy has revolved around her environmental anxiety and its impact on every area of her life. When she wakes up every day, she looks through her window to what she sees as a world in peril. She is personally pained by the manifold ways that humans are mistreating the planet. Even though she has everything she needs on a physical level, she often tells me that "If the environment isn't OK, then I'm just not OK." She feels intensely unsafe and unstable living in a world where a natural disaster could occur at any time, and where the future sustainability of human life seems so precarious. This particular client illuminated for me how the current state of the earth has changed the way in which some people orient to their personal future and even their individual sense of purpose. Where for many it appears to be a given truth that we are working towards a better future for the next generations, infusing our individual life with a larger sense of meaning, for this client the future was no longer something secure that she could hang her sense of meaning and fulfillment on.

Another client of mine always felt a strong sense that the meaning of his life had everything to do with becoming a father. Ever since he could remember he desired to be a dad, seeing parenthood as his greatest contribution to this life. When he learned more about global issues such as overpopulation and food scarcity, it seriously called into question whether having a child made sense for him anymore. His concern for the environment ignited a personal identity crisis as he contemplated who he would be and what he would do if having children no longer seemed viable or wise from an environmental perspective. His worry for the planet created a state of constant urgency in his internal nervous system and hypervigilance that disrupted his work and marriage.

With both of these clients, I found that by treating their attachment anxiety with the environment the same way I would work with relational attachment trauma, they were both able to rebuild an inner sense of safety and security. Each of them developed a larger felt sense of trust in the wisdom and support that the earth has to offer, while also feeling more empowered, rather than overwhelmed or complacent, about their environmental efforts.

Finally, in talking about the global level, it is also extremely important to highlight collective trauma. This is the traumatic impact that happens to societies over multiple generations when experiences including slavery, genocide, famine, war or the subjugation of women occur. The individuals who experience these events are undeniably impacted, but the effect also transcends the individual, altering the course of the world in unfathomable and incalculable ways. Thomas Hübl is the cofounder of the The Pocket Project, a nonprofit organization dedicated to the healing of collective trauma. He posits that we currently exist in a traumatized collective and the main symptom of being in a traumatized world is that we feel separate from each other, from the world, from spirit and from the natural world as a whole.[39] These symptoms are not just present in the collective or even individual psyches, but can become evident through actual changes in our genetic expression. Unresolved trauma from previous generations can alter the expression of DNA, making subsequent generations more susceptible to certain health issues, increased anxiety, PTSD and wariness to danger. This means that certain mental health or physical symptoms that you are experiencing today at the self level may have actually been inherited from collective traumas that your ancestors went through generations ago.

§

Traumas arise in many forms over multiple generations and how each person and their nervous system responds to the very same incident can vary greatly in degree. Trauma and attachment wounds separate us from feeling safe and secure, and left unaddressed they can create serious impairments in our ability to connect, respond or even function. All of these levels can cause threats, ruptures and violations that activate the attachment system. This means that each level has the potential to impact how safe we feel in our bodies, with others and in the world at large. Living in regular chaos, fear or uncertainty is not conducive to secure attachment. At each separate level we can look at a potential trauma occurring at that level and see how it then permeates to all of the levels above and below. Traumas that continue to occur at the levels of culture, society and the collective cannot entirely be healed by the individual, but that does not mean that they are beyond cleansing and repair at the self and relationship levels where we do have more power to take responsibility for our own healing. As I've already alluded to, healing is available to all of us at these different levels too. When ruptures occur at one level, we can focus our healing on that specific level, but we must also utilize the repair and respite that the other levels have to offer us—whether through self-compassion, a warm embrace from a loved one, a home where we can relax, being acknowledged and accepted within a community, receiving legal rights or benefits that were previously denied, or a quiet walk in nature to restore our inner equilibrium.

Part *Two*

Now that we have become more familiar with attachment theory and trauma, we will use Part Two to become better acquainted with consensual nonmonogamy. This section will address what consensual nonmongamy is, what attachment research has to say about nonmonogamy, why understanding attachment is particularly important for people practicing nonmonogamy, and how attachment ruptures and traumas can occur at multiple levels of the nested model of attachment and trauma when a person is nonmonogamous.

Part Two

CHAPTER FOUR
CONSENSUAL NONMONOGAMY

WE ARE LIVING IN A TIME OF NOTABLE CHANGE. Since change is the only constant, we could probably say that about any time in history, but over the last several decades, multiple established beliefs and deeply rooted cultural and societal practices have shifted. This includes attitudes towards race, class, gender and sexuality. While these societal revisions are far from complete and there is still much room for improvement, over the past 50 years or so marginalized groups have received more access, acknowledgment, justice and rights than previously granted in Western history. These necessary changes have come from the courageous and sustained efforts of the oppressed. Many people, known and unknown, have sacrificed their personal safety, their own freedoms and even their lives for the collective.

As lifestyles and biases previously invisible to the privileged have been exposed and deconstructed, choice has emerged. We have increased choice to pick what path in life we want to take, choice in how we identify ourselves and the choice of who and how we love. While transformations in constructs of race, class, gender and

sexual orientation have thus far been in the vanguard
of this societal change, monogamy has mostly stayed
unchallenged as a social construct, with those who do
not fit within its constraints finding themselves alienated
from a profound social revolution. As Esther Perel points
out,[40] even the monolith of the family has evolved with
the proliferation of alternatives to the nuclear family. The
emergence of stepfamilies, blended families, sperm and
egg donor families, single-parent families and surrogate
families have expanded our acceptance of what a family
can look like.

However, the romantic ideal of the monogamous
couple has mostly stayed intact as the dominant model
for love and relationships. Well, at least on the surface.
The divorce rate in the US is at 40 to 50 percent, and an
estimated 30 to 60 percent of married men and 20 to 50
percent of married women in the United States admit
to cheating on their partners.[41] Perel reminds us that
there is plenty of evidence that the monogamous model
doesn't necessarily work, with many people endorsing a
proclaimed monogamy, while actually performing *clan-
destine nonmonogamy.* And yet, despite this substantial
discrepancy between people espousing monogamy and
actually practicing it, its stronghold on the romantic
status quo is undeniable. Couple privilege and the bias of
monogamy are still omnipresent in both contemporary
American culture and at the global level. It is still predominantly believed that monogamy is not only the morally
superior way to practice partnership, but also the one and
only way to do so. This paradigm is so well-established
that straying from it often entails the risk of familial and
social estrangement, as well as an assortment of legal
repercussions, imprisonment or even death.

However, consensual nonmonogamy (CNM) is on the rise. Books like *Sex at Dawn* and *The Ethical Slut* remind us that even though monogamy is a relatively new concept in human history, CNM as a legitimate relationship option and an unconcealed lifestyle choice is still fairly new to our modern times. For decades, even centuries, partaking in relationships with multiple partners was relegated to underground events and communities. The sexual revolution of the 1960s brought CNM out of hiding, but awareness and acceptance of people practicing CNM was not instantaneous. Only in the last decade or two have we seen a substantial increase in the number of books published, academic research funded and media such as podcasts emerge with CNM as their focus. Today, we see CNM pop up in our newsfeeds, discussed in the media, portrayed on mainstream TV shows and offered as one of many relationship status options to choose from on dating apps and social media sites. Researcher Amy Moors found that there was a steady increase in the number of Google searches for terms related to polyamory and open relationships between 2006 and 2015.[42] Additionally, and tellingly, the American Psychological Association has created the Task Force on Consensual Non-Monogamy to promote awareness and inclusivity around CNM and non-traditional relationships.

CNM is unquestionably having its cultural moment, and it's not just a passing trend. Distinct from cheating, where sexual or romantic relations with more than one person are deceitful, consensual nonmonogamy is an umbrella term for the practice of simultaneously having multiple sexual or romantic partners where everyone involved is aware of and consents to the relationship structure. People practicing CNM value transparency, consent, open and honest communication, personal responsibility, autonomy, compassion, sex positivity and freedom for themselves and others. Moreover, people practicing CNM typically embrace the following ideas and principles: love is not possessive or a finite resource; it is normal to be attracted to more than one person at the same time; there are multiple ways to practice love, sexual and intimate relationships; and jealousy is *not* something to be avoided or feared, but something that can be informative and worked through. Mystic Life, author of *Spiritual Polyamory,* states, "This path requires owning jealousy as it arises, accepting others as they are, developing [one's] own sense of personal wholeness, and letting go of the belief that loving someone more means loving someone else less."[43]

Using two separate US Census samples, Haupert et al. found that over 20 percent of people in the United States admit to having participated in CNM at some point in their life, regardless of race, age, religion, class, political affiliation or level of education.[44] Other researchers estimate that 4 to 5 percent of people in the US are currently engaged in a CNM relationship.[45] That's over 16 million people. When comparing people in monogamous relationships to people in consensually nonmonogamous relationships, researchers have found that CNM relationships have similar levels of commitment, longevity, satisfaction, passion and love as monogamous relationships do.[46] Additionally, despite what people might presume, CNM relationships have also been found to have greater levels of trust and lower levels of jealousy than monogamous ones.[47]

Why Nonmonogamy?

Whenever I have an individual or a couple who are either already practicing CNM or about to begin their CNM journey in my office, one of my first questions is always "why?" I ask this to gain deeper understanding and in order to provide meaningful support, because as Simon Sinek advises,[48] it is through knowing our *why* for doing something—not just *what* we are doing and *how* we do it—that leads to success in our endeavors. My experience with nonmonogamous clients has shown me that the people who articulate their deeper purpose—that is, their *why* for being nonmonoga-mous—are then better able to navigate the ups and downs that lie ahead. When the waters of CNM begin to pick up and the emotional rapids of opening up your relationship begin, having your *why* to remember and return to can serve as the needed life jacket that keeps you and your relationship afloat. However, although two or more people want to practice CNM together—even two people in the same marriage—they may not have the same reasons for being nonmonogamous. Knowing why you want to practice nonmonogamy and how that might be similar to or different from your partners' reasons can better inform exactly what your version of nonmonogamy looks like together, including the agreements you make with different partners, and how you go about enacting CNM for yourself.

Moors, Matsick and Schechinger explored the dif-ferent relationship motivations and perceived benefits for people who engaged in CNM compared to people in monogamous relationships.[49] Both groups had the rela-tionship benefits of family, trust, love, sex, commitment and communication, regardless of whether they were in a monogamous or nonmonogamous relationship. However, people in CNM relationships additionally expressed having the distinct relationship benefits of increased need fulfillment, variety of nonsexual activities and personal growth. Instead of expecting one partner to meet all of their needs, people engaged in CNM felt that a major advantage of being nonmonogamous was the ability to have their different needs met by more than one person, as well as being able to experience a variety of nonsexual activities that one relationship may not fulfill. The other notable relationship benefit unique to people in CNM relationships was personal growth—people reported feeling that being nonmonogamous afforded them increased freedom from restriction, self and sexual expression and the ability to grow and develop. The authors of this research state that people in monogamous relationships may also experience such benefits, but these three benefits were mostly highlighted by people in CNM relationships, offering some potentially interesting insight into their motivations for participating in CNM.

When I ask my own clients why they are either considering CNM or already practicing nonmonogamy, most, if not all of them, respond in a way that agrees with these findings. They declare that they seek to have greater need fulfillment, want greater expression of themselves through the experiences and activities that will come from having multiple partners and say that they are interested in the personal growth and development that nonmonogamy inevitably catalyzes. Many people want to give and receive the additional love and support that come with having multiple partners. In addition to these reasons, I also see people consistently offer three other reasons for being nonmonogamous: sexual diversity, philosophical views and because CNM is a more authentic expression of who they are.

Let's explore these three reasons, starting with the sexual. It's not uncommon to hear someone who is trying to describe nonmonogamy to their family or friends, or speak about it in a professional or public setting, emphasize that CNM not just about the sex, but rather about the increased love, support and connection that come from having multiple partners. While this may very well be true, for many people, nonmonogamy is at least partly about the sex. And there's nothing wrong with that! I think that it's both well-intended and understandable that people say it isn't about sex, since research has shown that people tend to be significantly more uncomfortable with the idea of CNM relationships that emphasize sex over love than they are with CNM relationships that are based more on romantic and emotional connections.[50] We also intuitively know that telling our friends, parents or colleagues that we are in it for the love will probably fare better than telling them that we are in it for the sex. To me, this is an unfortunate symptomatic expression of our sex-negative culture that shames us for our basic human needs, desires and sexuality. There are people who genuinely need and want sexual diversity and it is not because they are sexually deviant, avoidantly attached, addicted to sex or noncommittal. Instead, they are people who embrace their sexuality and the diverse desires and expressions that it may encompass and require. There are also many couples who love each other deeply and have a wonderful partnership, but may have very different sexual needs. Perhaps they have different sexual styles, one partner being kinkier or more into BDSM than the other, or divergent sex drives or anatomical incompatibility. Some people find themselves in one of these situations and conclude that there is no reason to dismantle their entire life and give up their meaningful relationship because they want or need different things than their partner in the bedroom.

For people whose reason for engaging in nonmonogamy is philosophical, often this outlook arises from their readings or inquiries into the history of monogamy and its connection with patriarchal control over women's sexuality. These people feel that participating in such a relationship structure would be out of integrity with their values. Similarly, there are people who critically question traditional marriage and the imbalanced societal and cultural privileges it provides. They also report disliking the ever-increasing and impossible expectations that are placed on a life partner and that set many couples up for failure. Like the group of CNM people in the Moors et al. study who questioned if it is possible for one person to meet all of their needs, people are also questioning whether the institution of marriage is realistic and sustainable for them, with nonmonogamy stepping in as a preferable alternative.

The final motivation I see in my nonmonogamous clients is that people practice CNM because it just feels like this is who they are. For these people, nonmonogamy is not so much a lifestyle choice, as it is for some people, but rather an expression of their fundamental self. This group is more *nonmonogamous as orientation* than *nonmonogamous as lifestyle*. People who identify as nonmonogamous by lifestyle step into nonmonogamy as an intentional choice. They are often proud of and committed to this choice, but nonmonogamy in their case might be something that comes and goes depending on the partner or partners they are with, the phase of life they are in or their overall life circumstances. People who identify as nonmonogamous as orientation describe their nonmonogamy not as a choice, but as who they essentially are and how they are fundamentally wired. I often hear these people say that they feel most themselves when they are with multiple people, be it sexually or romantically. Some people who identify as nonmonogamous by orientation are fortunate enough to have been nonmonogamous from the time they started dating or being sexual. But many people come into their nonmonogamy orientation a bit later, often after having suffered from the belief that they are broken or defective in some way after struggling to be faithful to their partners or feeling that monogamy was never fully right for them.

The Different Types of Consensual Nonmonogamy

There are numerous ways that people practice non-monogamy and for every person, couple, triad, quad or polycule that says they are practicing a certain type of CNM, there are manifold ways that their version might be enacted. Even when people tell me the specific style of nonmonogamy they practice, I still ask, "what exactly does that look like for *you*?" There is no one right way to practice CNM and it is more of a "create your own relationship" than a one-size-fits-all approach, but there are still certain distinctions in the ways that people practice CNM that are important to name.

Each different style of CNM or CNM relationship structure will have different degrees of openness to sexual and/or emotional engagement with others, as well as different types of relationship agreements or rules. In Figure 4.1, I plot some of the main relationship structures or styles within CNM based on the two dimensions of emotional exclusivity and sexual exclusivity. On the horizontal axis, we find high emotional exclusivity on the left and low emotional exclusivity on the right. The vertical axis has high sexual exclusivity at the top and low sexual exclusivity at the bottom. Please note that these two dimensions are not the only way to comprehend the different types of CNM, so please take what helps and dismiss the rest. Additionally, although I place certain types of CNM in specific regions on this graph, there will always be exceptions to where someone else would plot their own version of that same type of CNM.

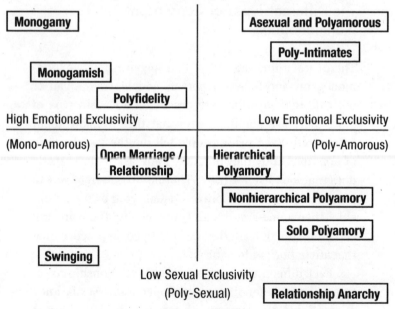

FIGURE 4.1: The different types of nonmonogamy.

Upper Left Quadrant

Monogamy: Monogamy is found in the upper left quadrant because it is traditionally high in both sexual and emotional exclusivity. Some couples that consider themselves monogamous do vary on how emotionally open or closed they are to people outside of the relationship, but it is common for monogamous couples to consider each other as their only sexual partner and emotional primary. In monogamous couples, a partner is usually considered to be cheating if they engage sexually with another and/ or if they share deep or romantic emotions with others.

Monogamish: Coined by sex columnist Dan Savage, this term refers to couples who are mostly sexually and emotionally exclusive, but periodically engage in extramarital or extra-relational sex or sexual play. These exceptions might include occasional one-time hookups, sex with others while traveling apart, or even kissing other people at certain types of events.

Polyfidelity: A romantic or sexual relationship that involves more than two people, but these people are exclusive with each other. This could include a group relationship of three or more people that is closed to any additional outside partners, or it could be a person who has more than one partner and their partners are not dating each other, but they are also closed to additional relationships.

Lower Left Quadrant

Swinging: The practice of couples engaging in sexual activity with other couples, individuals or groups. The focus of those encounters is primarily sexual rather than romantic or emotionally intimate and couples who consider themselves as swingers typically sexually play with others while they are together in the same room or at the same event, rather than completely separately from each other. In my practice, I've encountered many swingers who do want to feel some level of connection with the people they are swinging with, but often prefer to keep emotional involvement to a minimum in order to maintain the emotional primacy of their marriage or primary relationship.

Open Marriage/Relationship: A relationship where one or both partners in a relationship have sexual or romantic relationships outside of their primary partnership. Open relationships tend to be more focused on having sex and limiting the degree of emotional involvement with others in order to keep the primary, dyadic relationship as the first priority.

Lower Right Quadrant

Polyamory: The practice of having many (*poly*) loves (*amory*), where everyone involved is aware and consenting of partners simultaneously having multiple romantic and sexual relationships. People who identify as polyamorous tend to focus on the falling in love part of being nonmonogamous, where the intention of having multiple partners is to be in love and have multiple emotionally invested relationships. People practicing polyamory can differ in the degree to which they implement hierarchy in their different relationships.

Hierarchical Polyamory: A subset of polyamory where there is a ranking system among romantic/sexual relationships and some relationships are considered more important than others. A person's primary partner(s) would be at the top of this ranking system since primaries usually cohabitate, share resources, make decisions together and organize their schedules so that they are spending the most amount of time together. Hierarchical relationships tend to use the terms primary, secondary, and sometimes tertiary, describing various levels of importance, commitment and who has the rights to create relationship agreements. Typically, the people in a primary relationship with each other set the rules for all subsequent relationships, which might include restrictions on certain recreational or social activities, limits on certain sex acts or on how strong, deep or invested other relationships can become. Many polyamory experts caution against hierarchical relationship structures that create asymmetrical balances of power in which people in secondary or tertiary positions have little or no say about how their relationship unfolds, or are subject to vetoes or rules from their metamours.

In *More Than Two*, Franklin Veaux and Eve Rickert make the distinction between *prescriptive* and *descriptive* hierarchy.[51] Prescriptive hierarchy occurs when a couple predetermines that their status as primaries will not change and all future relationships will be subordinate to theirs. All of the relationship styles in the lower left side of this chart could be described as being hierarchical forms of consensual nonmonogamy and in the upper left quadrant, hierarchy would be assumed. Descriptive hierarchy is less about a given relationship prescription for the future. The term describes a hierarchy that might include several primaries that have emerged more organically and have become more domestically, financially or emotionally entangled than other relationships, but there is still an openness to things changing or new people entering the hierarchy.

Nonhierarchical Polyamory: The practice of having multiple simultaneous relationships without imposing hierarchies. This means that there is no ranking system of primary and secondary. It means that no one person has extra influence over a person's relationships, including veto power or more privilege because they live together or have been together longer. All important people get a seat at the table and everyone gets to have a voice. Each relationship is allowed to grow into what it naturally wants to be. In some cases, nonhierarchical polyamory may include prioritization of certain relationships in instances where people have children together or live together, but the nonhierarchical structure does not endorse power differentials and allows for more flexibility in how relationships can change and evolve over time.

Solo Polyamory: An approach to polyamory that emphasizes personal agency. Individuals do not seek to engage in relationships that are tightly couple-centric or financially and/or domestically entwined. People who identify as solo poly emphasize autonomy, the freedom to choose their own relationships without seeking permission from others, and flexibility in the form their relationships take. It is a common misconception that people practicing solo polyamory are either more casual or less committed in their relationships, but this is not necessarily the case. Solo poly folks can be deeply emotionally involved and committed in their relationships, but they typically choose not to take on the traditional roles that some partners assume like living together, having shared bank accounts or doing each other's laundry (at least not as a relationship obligation). One principle of solo poly that I think everyone can benefit from is the notion of being your own primary partner and prioritizing your relationship with yourself first and foremost.

Relationship Anarchy: This type of CNM falls at the very end or even off this chart completely. The term was first coined in 2006 by Andie Nordgren,[52] who applied political anarchist principles to interpersonal relationships. Relationship anarchists seek to dismantle the social hierarchies dictating how sexual and romantic relationships are prioritized over all other forms of love, and so people who identify as relationship anarchists make less distinction between the importance or value of their lovers over their friends or other people in their life, and they do not only reserve intimacy or romance for the people they have sex with.

Upper Right Quadrant

Poly Intimates: I've started to use this term for people who are sexually exclusive with one partner, but who are not emotionally exclusive with that partner in ways that a traditional monogamous relationship would typically disallow, be suspicious of or characterize as emotional cheating. Poly intimates might share varying degrees of romance and emotional intimacy with more than just the person they are sexually exclusive with. Poly intimates might be nonsexual partners who live together, travel together, raise children together or share other aspects of life, where the level of investment and involvement does not fit the conventional notion of friendship.

Polyamorous and Asexual: People who identify as asexual (or Aces) experience little to no sexual attraction to others. Aces may or may not experience romantic attraction, and Aces may or may not choose to engage in sex or romance. Placement in this quadrant is specifically referring to people who identify as nonsexual asexual and romantically polyamorous. Since asexuality can vary greatly in how attraction, sexuality, arousal and romance are experienced, Aces may find that other placements on this chart are better suited to them.

§

In this chapter, I acknowledged that nonmonogamy is not a new form of relationship, but that it is currently becoming more common. I examined the reasons why people engage in nonmonogamy based on survey research and what I've also seen in my own psychotherapy and coaching practice. I also covered the different ways that people can express being nonmonogamous based on how sexually exclusive or sexually nonexclusive they are intersecting with how emotionally exclusive or emotionally nonexclusive they are. After reading this chapter, which of the reasons for being nonmonogamous resonate with you? Do you have reasons for being nonmonogamous that weren't mentioned here? In looking at the different types of nonmonogamy, what did you learn about yourself or your partners? And are there other ways that you would define your version of nonmonogamy?

CHAPTER FIVE
ATTACHMENT AND NONMONOGAMY

ATTACHMENT RESEARCH AND RESOURCES for consensually nonmonogamous relationships are scarce. It is safe to say that the field of attachment theory is highly mononormative. The overwhelming majority of research conducted to understand adult romantic attachment is undertaken with monogamous couples, and advice about how to establish a secure attachment either assumes monogamy or outright prescribes monogamy as a necessary precondition for establishing safety and security. Moors, Conley, Edelstein and Chopik state that "attachment theory presumes that healthy, satisfying relationships are, by definition, dyadic."[53] Authors on attachment theory will assert that being pair-bonded is the prototype for attachment in adulthood, that couples need to create a *couple bubble* around them in order to ensure security, and that your partner needs to be the one, single or main person that you emotionally depend on. I question if these criteria are even healthy from a monogamous standpoint (a considerable amount of the mono-romantic ideal can actually be codependency in disguise), but at the very least we can see how these ideas and assumptions within the field of attachment are excluding people in CNM relationships.

What attachment researchers say about the relationship between sex and attachment creates another mononormative problem for people in CNM relationships. Attachment literature unquestionably has important insights into how the different attachment styles experience and relate to sex.[54] Differences in motivation and experiences are to be expected and are not inherently a problem, but some behaviors such as casual sex, one-night stands, sex outside of marriage, multiple sexual partners, partaking in bondage, voyeurism, exhibitionism and even sexting are all associated with insecure attachment. The problem gets even bigger when people then take these research findings a step further and conclude that since these sexual behaviors are the types of behaviors that nonmonogamous people participate in, then nonmonogamy must in and of itself be an expression of insecure attachment. Just to be clear, I am not saying this and, as you will see below, the current research on CNM relationships does not support this, but many of my clients have unfortunately heard previous therapists equate being CNM with attachment insecurity and pathologize them for their lifestyle and sexuality. In such cases, it is important to distinguish between the intentions behind specific sexual behaviors instead of just looking at the sex act itself. If someone is pursuing multiple partners to avoid intimacy or using sex in an attempt to secure intimacy when they feel insecure, then in those cases such behaviors can be seen as an expression of insecure attachment. But many people engage in these very same behaviors from a secure place, where they are able to have multiple sex partners, one-night stands or BDSM play in intentional, highly attuned, connected and meaningful ways.

When we start to dig into the current research on CNM and attachment, we find the research is extremely limited. As I write this book in 2020, there are less than a handful of studies that examine the relationship between attachment and CNM. From a research perspective, this is insufficient. The good news is that what little research has been done thus far demonstrates that people in CNM relationships are just as likely to be securely attached as people in monogamous relationships. In a survey conducted with over 1,300 people, Moors, Conley, Edelstein and Chopik examined whether there were any differences in attachment styles for people who were either in monogamous, swinging or polyamorous relationships.[55] They found that there was no difference in attachment anxiety levels between people who were monogamous versus those that were CNM, and that people in CNM relationships were actually lower in attachment avoidance than the people in monogamous relationships were. This research suggests that people in CNM relationships exhibit characteristics of secure attachment, maybe even more so than people in monogamous relationships. A smaller study of 179 gay men similarly found no difference in attachment styles between the participants who were in in monogamous relationships and those in nonmonogamous relationships.[56] A 2014 doctoral dissertation investigated whether there was any difference in the attachment styles of people who identified as polyamorous compared to people who identified as monogamous and found that there was no statistically significant difference in attachment-related anxiety or avoidance between the two groups.[57]

In a 2019 study, Moors, Ryan and Chopick examined the attachment styles of over 350 polyamorous people who were currently in at least two different relationships.[58] They found that people practicing polyamory exhibited secure attachment styles with both of their partners and, interestingly, having more of an insecure style with one specific partner did not affect the attachment functioning of their other relationships. Similar to how a child can be securely attached to one parent, while simultaneously insecurely attached to another parent, polyamorous adults can have different attachment styles with different romantic partners that are independent of each other. While the current research on CNM and attachment is encouraging, the shortage of studies to reference creates a massive gap in the current attachment literature, as well as many unanswered questions about the relationship between attachment and CNM.

When it comes to advice on how to cultivate secure attachment in nonmonogamous relationships, the literature is practically nonexistent. Some nonmonogamous bloggers and podcasters have used their platforms to educate audiences about the different attachment styles as something beneficial to be aware of in nonmonogamous relationships, but the conversation usually ends there. The only literature I could find on anything related to how to create a secure attachment in CNM relationships is an online article by Clinton Power titled "How Secure Functioning Can Help Polyamorous Couples."[59] The article is geared towards therapists working with polyamorous couples and it explains how to work with these couples based on Stan Tatkin's Psychobiological Approach to Couple Therapy (PACT). The PACT method is well-researched and has been designed to help adult romantic relationships securely function. In the article, Power uses a case example of a married heterosexual couple in an open marriage. The wife is struggling because the husband is experiencing an increase in feelings and intensity with his secondary partner. Power proposes that the couple is struggling because they are breaking several of the secure functioning PACT principles, which advise us that CNM couples should:

- Put your primary relationship first before all other relationships.
- Have clear relationship boundaries that support the health of the primary relationship.
- Go to your primary partner first with important news or life events.
- Manage thirds (meaning the third person, or in this case the secondary partner) to protect the primacy of the main relationship.
- Never threaten the security of the primary relationship.
- Resolve conflict by finding solutions that work for both partners.

When I present the suggestions from this article to an audience at CNM conferences, the room usually starts to rumble with disapproving laughs, grunts and even boos. Before offering my own opinion, I ask the audience to tell me what they think about these suggestions. The first critique that people usually offer is that this article promotes a very hierarchical version of polyamory that puts the couple in a position of power over the secondary partner, who would have no rights or say in the boundaries that were set or the solutions that were created, even though they directly impact her and the relationship she is in. People in the audience are often also irritated by how this article only speaks to one version of CNM, which might work for people practicing hierarchical polyamory or open marriage, but that completely overlooks people who are solo poly, nonhierarchical polyamory or relationship anarchist. When the audience contains experienced therapists or coaches who work with nonmonogamous couples, they will also often add that part of the issue here is that this couple is functioning from two different forms of nonmonogamy (the wife wanting more of an open marriage style of nonmonogamy and the husband being more polyamourous in his approach), and that the article is encouraging them to take on her style over his without deeper discussion.

In addition to the feedback that the audience has to offer, my critique of this article is that it is relying too much on the structure of the relationship to ensure and safeguard secure attachment instead of the quality of relating between partners to forge secure attachment. When we rely on the structure of our relationship, whether that is through being monogamous with someone or practicing hierarchical forms of CNM, we run the risk of forgetting that secure attachment is an embodied expression built upon how we consistently respond and attune to each other, not something that gets created through structure and hierarchy. Secure attachment is created through the quality of experience we have with our partners, not through the notion or the fact of either being married or being a primary partner. The narratives people have about love, marriage, primary partnership and how to achieve relationship security are powerful, so much so that just the idea of being in love, married or in a primary partnership can lead us to think we are experiencing attachment security when in reality we might not be. We often assume that having more structural ties in a relationship means more security. In some cases it does, but as the high rates of divorce and cheating demonstrate, even a monogamous marriage that typically represents the pinnacle of relationship security is not necessarily any more secure than other forms of relationship. People can commit to being married for life, but still feel universes away from the person they share a bed with. Two people can consider each other primary partners but still experience relational neglect even though they might technically be able to wield veto power over other partners or have first choice on how holidays are spent. Relationship structure does not guarantee emotional security.

I've witnessed many couples who have measured their sense of personal and relationship security based on the fact of having shared finances, being legally married, running a business together, co-owning a home or how many carats the engagement ring has. These more structural demonstrations of security can be signs of genuine commitment and they undoubtedly make it more difficult for someone to just pick up and leave one day, but they do not ensure the high-quality attunement, presence and responsiveness that foster secure attachment at the interpersonal level. Here are some signs that might indicate that you are relying more on the structure of your relationship for your attachment and security than the emotional experience of your relationship:

- You theoretically know your partner loves you and is ultimately committed to you, your marriage and/ or your family, but you don't feel personally valued, seen or cherished.

- You share many forms of structural commitment with your partner, but don't have emotional or sexual intimacy (and one or both of you is not OK with that).
- When you ask your spouse or partner for more of their time or affection they get defensive and point out all of the professional, financial or domestic things that they do to show their commitment.
- You often feel alone in your relationship even though you live together or are around each other a lot.
- You or your partner defer to gender stereotypes to make the absence of certain forms of emotional or sexual connection more tolerable, such as "that's just how men are" or "well you know how women can be."
- In your relationship, the ideal of the marriage or the greater purpose of the family have become more important than the direct experience of how you treat each other.
- You're married or in primary partnership, but feel like you're always getting the short end of the stick when it comes to your spouse or partner's time, affection and attention.
- You know your partner is committed to you, but you don't know if they actually like and enjoy being with you.

If you experience any of these things I suggest working with your partner or partners to strengthen the emotional experience of your secure attachment, which is covered in Part Three. As I address in the next chapter, I've seen the dangers of people depending on the structure of their relationship to feel safe together. When they change that structure, either through opening up from monogamy or transitioning to a less hierarchical form of CNM, it can expose relational insecurities that were disguised by the pseudo or contrived security acquired from the previous relationship structure. The takeaway message here is not to abolish all relationship hierarchies or shared bank accounts, but instead for people to procure secure attachment from their relational experiences instead of their relationship structures. Allow your direct experience with a partner to be the vehicle to secure attachment instead of having certain relationship concepts, narratives or structures be the vehicle. When our experience with a partner is the route to secure attachment, we might still want certain relationship structures, benchmarks and milestone experiences, but the urgency at which we define, solidify or need to nail things down can relax and occur more organically.

Current research and resources about attachment and consensual nonmonogamy are scarce and at an embryonic stage. I am hopeful that more research and resources will continue to crop up as awareness and acceptance of nonmonogamy continues to grow, but for many people it will not be soon enough. Part Three is designed to walk you through the different components of secure functioning, not based on your relationship structure, but based on the behaviors that you can apply to any of your CNM relationships in which you seek to deepen polysecurity.

CHAPTER SIX

THE IMPORTANCE OF ATTACHMENT IN CONSENSUAL NONMONOGAMY

TO START, LET ME SAY that secure attachment with multiple romantic partners *is* possible. Honestly, it's really a necessity to do CNM well and thrive, but we'll get to that. Just as children do not only bond with one attachment figure, adults do and can have multiple securely attached relationships. When secure functioning is at play within CNM relationships, partners communicate well, trust each other, stick to their agreements and discuss wanted changes. They tend to have more compersion for their partners, they act respectfully towards their metamours and while they still do experience jealousy or envy, they are also able to support each other in the process. Jealousy becomes an opportunity for increased clarity and connection and it doesn't take them or their relationships down. When I talk to CNM folks who are securely attached, they may admit that their relationships require work and acknowledge that they are not always easy (more people means more complexity, and scheduling is always going to be an issue), but they also describe an underlying sense of ease within and throughout their relationships. When people are securely attached, they enjoy each other and the process of living as consensually nonmonogamous.

My experience with CNM clients has taught me an enormous amount about how and why understanding CNM through an attachment lens is so important. As CNM individuals and couples began to seek my counsel, I began to notice two distinct camps: those who were mostly thriving and those who seemed to be barely surviving. For those who were thriving, our work was often short-term. As these people entered into a new relationship paradigm, they reached out to me for some support, guidance and perspective. They usually quickly expressed that they had got what they came for. Now better able to implement their CNM journey, they moved merrily along their way. Every few months, I'd even receive a text or email with photos of their entire smiling polycule around a kitchen table (I kid you not!). These people still reached out for therapy or coaching sessions once in a while due to break-ups, STI scares, uncharted CNM situations to figure out and relationship transitions to process, but overall, CNM was working for them. They expressed feeling secure, and from my perspective they were enacting their multiple romantic partnerships, as well as their metamour relationships, from a place of secure functioning.

I call these people who thrive with their multiple partners *polysecure*. This is the state of being both securely attached to multiple romantic partners and having enough internal security to be able to navigate the structural relationship insecurity inherent to nonmonogamy, as well as the increased complexity and uncertainty that occurs when having multiple partners and metamours. More succinctly, being polysecure is having secure attachment with yourself and your multiple partners. Polysecure people are functioning securely both interpersonally and intrapersonally, both of which will be examined in more detail in Part Three.

There may be some people who enter nonmonogamy and are able to be polysecure right off the bat, but for many people this is not the case. All of my clients want to be secure within their selves and with their partners, but often the reality of nonmonogamy is too complicated, painful, dramatic, confusing and even traumatizing. These people transition to nonmonogamy and feel more polyinsecure than polysecure. For some of the individuals and couples I've worked with, their CNM struggles mirror the relationship challenges they encountered when previously monogamous, but many people are surprised, even shocked, by the issues they face because they are so unlike their monogamous past. Among couples who transition from monogamy to polyamory, many had healthy, secure monogamous relationships together and can't make sense of why they are now having so many communication problems, misunderstandings or fights despite their best efforts to be clear and loving with each other. Some of these couples feel as if they are falling apart at the seams. For many, the transition to poly (whether solo or with a partner) brings up forms of insecurity, anxiety and even panic attacks that they may not have experienced before. It is not uncommon for me to hear people say that they theoretically want to be poly, but emotionally they don't know if they can do it because they feel like they are losing their mind.

People struggling with a transition from monogamy to CNM may also find themselves without practical support from their friends, family and community. Sometimes, the people closest to them, even therapists, advise these struggling couples or individuals to go back to being monogamous. I have heard such couples receive advice that sounds something like, "Well, if you're struggling more in your relationship or with yourself now that you're polyamorous, you should just go back to being monogamous and everything will be OK again."

To me, telling people who are struggling with the transition from monogamy to CNM to go back to monogamy because CNM is just too difficult would be like telling the new parents of an infant who are struggling without sleep or personal time that maybe they should just send the kid back since they didn't have any of these issues before the child arrived. This analogy may seem ridiculous because you literally can't send the kid back, but that can be exactly what it can feel like for people who have made the transition out of monogamy into CNM, especially for people who experience CNM not as a lifestyle choice but as who they fundamentally are. Culturally, we know better than to tell people to give their kids away when they're struggling with the realities of parenthood. We also know not to tell a person who is struggling with the realities of coming out as lesbian, gay, bisexual or transgender that they should just go back to being straight or go back to being their birth gender since being LGBT in a mostly straight and gender-binarized world is just too hard. But when it comes to CNM, our well-intentioned friends, family and even helping professionals do not necessarily know better and they can be quick to point the finger at CNM as the problem. This mindset is often fueled by the fear that if a couple opens up their relationship, it is inevitable that they will then break up or get divorced. Even though many couples stay together after opening up, it is true that many will eventually split up. But relationships do not end because CNM was the problem or the cause of relationship struggles, but because of the experience of a major relationship paradigm shift that can create so much tumult.

Going from monogamy to CNM means that people are taking on a massive shift in their world view. Almost every aspect of love, romance, sex, partnership and family now has a different set of expectations, practices, codes of conduct and even language compared to the dominant monogamous paradigm of relationships. Deconstructing monogamy for yourself, with all of its ingrained beliefs and behaviors that you may have been practicing for your entire life, can be extremely difficult. The science of change has much to tell us about the necessary time and effort it takes to break habits, rewire beliefs and integrate into different paradigms based on new and different realities. Even when people identify as nonmonogamous as orientation and the transition might feel like a homecoming, there can still be deep-seated internalized polyphobia to work through.

Furthermore, when couples transition to CNM from a monogamous relationship together, there is the added layer of also deconstructing and reconstructing not just yourself, but your relationship as well. When you've shared years or even decades with someone in a monogamous identity together, this can be a particularly arduous transformation process and not every couple survives it. The paradigm shift can expose all of the underground issues that a relationship already had brewing and that would have eventually ended the relationship anyway. In these cases, the shift to CNM just expedited that process. Or a relationship might have been perfectly healthy and stable, but the transformational process of entering a new relationship paradigm changes one or both partners to the point that staying together is no longer what they genuinely want. I also see couples who definitely want to stay together but since they have little to no support in navigating the paradigm shift, they wind up losing each other, drowning in the process.

Over the past few years, there are increasingly more resources available for people transitioning to CNM. These materials have a predominant focus on helping individuals or couples figure out what type of CNM works best for them, how to design relationship agreements, practice safer sex, communicate better and how to manage jealousy. These are extremely important topics, and in many ways they are foundational to doing CNM well, but I've seen people come to my office struggling with agreements that have been broken, communication that isn't working or jealousy that seems immutable. Within several sessions we usually find that these are not the main issues but actually symptoms of other, deeper challenges that are arising from the change to CNM. If we are going to point the finger at a cause of distress, it is not nonmonogamy itself, but rather the paradigm shift that people try to navigate without a map to guide them through to the other side.

In a talk titled "Couples Transitioning from Monogamy to Polyamory," I highlight six challenges that I see emerge in the paradigm shift from monogamy to polyamory (they are also applicable to people transitioning from other forms of CNM, such as swinging or open relationships, to polyamory, especially when transitioning into nonhierarchical polyamory or solo polyamory). These challenges are:

1. Resistance to the paradigm shift itself. People want to change the structure of their relationship but don't actually want the relationship itself to change and grow in the ways needed to make the paradigm shift.

2. Insufficient skills. The skills and abilities that people used to keep their relationship healthy and happy in monogamy are no longer sufficient in a nonmonogamous context, so couples find themselves with only a percentage of the skills they need to be healthy, happy and functional in the paradigm of polyamory.

3. Couples never decoupled or went through healthy differentiation before they transitioned. Much of the mono-romantic ideal encourages forms of codependency, which can remain invisible and even functional for a couple until they **open up**. It is commonly believed and culturally reinforced that your partner completes you, that your identity should be fused with your partner or the relationship and that your partner is the main source of meaning, love and happiness in your life. True intimacy does not come from enmeshment, but from two differentiated individuals sharing themselves with each other. Trying to practice nonmonogamy while still enmeshed with a partner can cause much strife for you and anyone new you are trying to date.

4. One partner being more nonmonogamous in orientation and the other partner identifying as nonmonogamous as a lifestyle choice. The difference in pursuing CNM from a lifestyle choice versus an orientation usually influences how each person moves forward with and approaches

CNM. This difference can cause conflicts, hurt and many misunderstandings.

5. The paradigm shift creates an awakening of the self, where what was previously unexpressed and unrealized is now awakening in someone, potentially turning their entire world and relationships upside down. People may not just be waking up to their nonmonogamous desires or orientation, but also aspects of their sexuality, important identities or forms of oppressions that have previously been denied, exiled or completely unacknowledged.

6. An attachment crisis gets catalyzed from the transition into nonmonogamy.

I've found that the first four points, once identified, are relatively simple to address and move forward from. The last two points are more complicated and typically need more time and attention to address. The fifth point of how to recover and reinvent yourself when you are going through an awakening of the self—what I also call a *crisis of deconstruction*—requires more attention than I can allot here, since the focus of this book is the sixth point of how transitioning from monogamy to CNM impacts our attachment.

I've observed that the attachment changes in a person's relationship(s) that occur from becoming nonmonogamous are at the foundation of struggles with being CNM (as well as any previous insecure attachment traumas that can get brought into their relationships). Attempting to do CNM with an insecure attachment style or having attachment insecurity arise as a result of becoming nonmonogamous can seriously disrupt a person's sense of self, as well as their inner and outer safety in ways that can feel unbearable and be unsustainable. When transitioning into nonmonogamy there are several different ways that people experience challenges with their attachment system. Knowing where your specific attachment challenges stem from is an important part in healing. Addressing the cause can help you move from being polyinsecure to polysecure. Here are the ways that I see attachment disruptions occur in CNM:

Going CNM can expose your individual attachment insecurity.

For some people, monogamy can serve as a stand-in for actual secure attachment. Since the rules and structure of monogamy are so well-known and so strongly rein-forced, many times all you have to do is fall back on the structure of monogamy itself to create a sense of safety in a relationship. The very fact of being monogamously exclusive, verbally committed or legally married can be sufficient enough for some people to feel secure in the relationship. When these people then remove the struc-ture of monogamy by going nonmonogamous, their own insecure attachment style can get exposed. In such cases, being monogamous shielded the partners from having to face their own insecure attachment history. They may have been somewhat aware of their painful past, but being in a committed monogamous partnership was enough to assuage their own attachment insecurity. Once the security blanket of monogamy is lifted, these people are flooded with the pains of their insecure attachment past, as well as awareness of the ways they were actually relying on, even clinging to, monogamy to feel secure within themselves and in their relationship.

Monogamy can also buffer us from our own personal insecurities. These may or may not be attachment-based, but can be rooted in relational and cultural traumas or anxieties about our achievements, looks, intellectual abilities, likability, etc. When we commit to a long-term monogamous partnership or get married, these insecurities may still show up every now and again, but many of them get eclipsed by the very fact that we have someone who has devoted themselves to us, someone who we think will love us and stay with us no matter how pimply our butt gets, no matter how much our body changes or no matter how stained and worn-out our underwear becomes. In such cases, our self-esteem and sense of self-worth are contingent on our partner being monogamously committed to us instead of anchored in our own internal sense of self-worth, self-love and self-esteem. When people have depended on their partner's exclusivity for their own self-confidence, going nonmonogamous can pop the cork on all of their personal insecurities, making it painfully difficult to manage the fears and threats that surface in relation to what it means for them or their partner to be dating again.

Examples of signs that your transition to CNM has exposed your own attachment insecurity:

- You intellectually want to be nonmonogamous, but you're having trouble with emotionally getting on board.

- Even though your partner has been wonderful about meeting enough of your relationship needs and is doing a good job reassuring you that you matter to them, you still experience a roller-coaster of anxiety before and/or during the time they spend with other people, or you start to withdraw to protect yourself.

- You intellectually want to feel compersion for your partner having positive experiences with others, but you keep interpreting them being with others as a sign of your deficiency.
- After opening up, you are flooded with many of your childhood experiences and/or past traumas.
- After opening up, you realized that you have patterns of emotional/relational avoidance or codependency.

Going CNM can expose attachment insecurity in the relationship that is opening up.

In the same way that monogamy can mitigate personal attachment insecurities, it can also conceal attachment insecurities that are relationally based. As a couple opens up from a monogamous relationship, they usually perceive themselves as having been healthy and secure together. But, as the structure of monogamy is lifted, issues in the relationship that the couple didn't have to face before can appear, or issues that were ignored or tolerated can no longer be ignored or tolerated in the new structure of nonmonogamy. On both this point and the previous point, I see people depending on the relationship structure for their security instead of their actual relational experience with their partner. When the structure is removed, they are faced with all of the ways that the relationship was not functioning.

CNM is inherently insecure.

Unlike the built-in security that can ostensibly come from being monogamous, CNM is a relationship structure that is inherently insecure. In CNM, we don't have the security of knowing that a partner is with us because they see us as the best, one or only partner out there for them. In CNM we may not be the only or first person that our partner turns to or the last one they say goodnight to. In CNM we are less likely to meet new partners when they or we are single and able to create a new life together. Instead, we often have to figure out how to fit together alongside pre-existing structures and commitments with other partners. Furthermore, in CNM we are opening ourselves up to people who could become game changers for us or for our partner. Of course, game changers arise in monogamous relationships too, but in CNM we are *intentionally* going out to open our hearts and our bodies to more and different people who can potentially shake up our other relationships in unforeseen ways. Also, and importantly, in CNM we don't have all of the cultural and institutionalized support that our society has created for the monogamous couple.

The insecurity in CNM can actually be a *good* thing in that it can keep us from taking our partners for granted or becoming complacent in our relationships in ways that are often found in monogamous relationships. Personally, I find security in the fact that when I'm in CNM relationships I know that my partners are not with me because they are obliged to be, but because they continue to choose to be. However, the inherent insecurity in CNM relationships can be grinding. This form of relationship can bring up levels of uncertainty that many people are not yet equipped for, especially when they don't have enough internal secure attachment. To create sustainable healthy relationships with multiple partners, it's crucial to learn how to build polysecurity in your CNM relation-ships and even more so to cultivate secure attachment and equanimity within yourself.

Having multiple partners can replicate the conditions of attachment insecurity.

For many of us, our lives are complicated and over-scheduled. The baseline maintenance of life has grown beyond what previous generations had to manage. Many of us juggle multiple life factors including businesses to run, work to go to, children to take care of, our physical bodies to tend to, homes and cars that need maintenance, friends and family to keep up with, groups and communities to stay active with, emails to respond to and an online presence to maintain. Not to mention the time needed for self-care, exercise, play, personal growth, meditation practice, shows to binge or simple quiet time in nature. Economic times have also changed. For many, a single income is barely enough to support a single person, let alone a family. As I enumerate all of these life factors, I'm actually surprised anyone has time for even one securely attached relationship. Secure attachment takes time, both to establish and to maintain. Research shows that it takes babies up to seven months for their attachment to their caregivers to become securely established, and for adults, a securely attached romantic relationship takes approximately two years to really solidify.[60] So, while you might feel an instant resonance or connection with someone, building an actual relationship based on trust, seeing each other in multiple contexts, deeply under-standing each other and relating in securely attached ways requires time.

I want to make an important distinction here that we will return to again. In CNM, it is not necessary for all of our relationships to be attachment-based. There is a difference between being in a secure connection with someone and having a securely attached relationship. Secure connections are with people or partners who we don't have daily or regular contact with, but with whom we know that when we reach out it will feel as if a moment hasn't passed. We are secure in the bond that we have with such people, and this bond might be immensely meaningful, special and important to us, but it's not necessarily a relationship that requires us to invest regular maintenance and attention. In CNM, these might be the partners we refer to as comets, satellites or casual. They're the people who we see at special events a few times a year or our less-involved long-distance relationships. Securely attached relationships are based on consistency and reliability. These are the people who are there for each other in responsive and attuned ways more times than not. They are our "go-to" people who have our back and to whom we can turn when we feel hurt or threatened and or need support, comfort or reassurance. They're the people we are excited to share our latest news or discoveries with. Sue Johnson simplifies what we are looking for in our attachment relationships through the three questions: are you available, are you responsive, are you emotionally engaged?[61]

I have seen a frequent phenomenon in CNM relationships that are more attachment-based: as partners begin to spend more time with other people, the conditions that create increased attachment insecurity can emerge. As discussed in Chapter One, the main factor in a child developing an anxious attachment pattern is inconsistent attunement from their primary caregiver—there is love, but it is unreliable. In CNM, as people begin to go on more dates, enter into additional relationships or experience new relationship energy with someone else, they can start to become less available, responsive or attuned to their pre-existing partners. The person experiencing an increase in their number of partners or a deepening in a specific relationship may not intend to give less to their other partners (often they think they can manage all their relationships to a high degree), but due to the limits of how many hours there are in a day, how many date nights there are in a week or how many people you can text with at once, splitting time among more and more people can create insecure conditions for their other partners. The person with a new partner has now become (intentionally or not) more inconsistent, unpredictable and inaccessible to their attachment-based relationships than they were previously.

The partners who are receiving less time and attention will usually begin to feel uneasy, anxious or angry, and they will begin to protest. As they begin to voice their dissatisfaction that their partner is being less available, present or connected than the partner used to be, they may be told they are too jealous or needy. But their protest can actually be a healthy sign of their attachment system detecting too much disconnection and therefore acting up in order to course-correct. It's the body's inner guidance system indicating that important needs are going unmet. The insecurities arising for the partner who feels left out, left behind or no longer as important are not necessarily manifestations of jealousy. Rather, the situation and the relationship they find themselves in are no longer providing them with the same degree of attachment-based needs fulfillment that they have become accustomed to, triggering a more hyperactivated anxious preoccupied style. In such cases, sometimes just the awareness of what is going on can be enough for the partner who has been less attentive to re-engage. Other times, strategies for being less polysaturated and more present with each partner need to be implemented, or sometimes renegotiations about the level of involvement or commitment of the relationship are needed.

Similarly, the conditions that contribute to a disorganized attachment pattern can also arise in nonmonogamous relationships. In situations where nonmonogamy is not done ethically, where people are subject to vetoes or to decisions and boundaries that they did not co-create, and when relationship agreements or safe sex practices are being repeatedly broken, a person's safety and security alarms bells can go off in ways that become highly dysregulating and damaging. In any relationship, whether monogamous or nonmonogamous, abuse, neglect, aggression, violence, manipulation, control or gaslighting can also contribute to a fearful-avoidant attachment experience where the one you love and trust is also the one you fear and shouldn't really trust.

The conditions that breed a disorganized attachment adaptation are not specific to CNM by any means, but I have seen a variation that is unique to CNM. There can be something very disorienting that happens for some new CNM couples who were first monogamous together and were accustomed to being each other's main source of comfort, support and relief from distress. As the relationship opens, a partner's actions with other people (even ethical ones that were agreed upon) can become a source of distress and pose an emotional threat. Everything that this person is doing with other people can become a source of intense fear and insecurity for their pre-existing partner, catapulting them into the paradoxical disorganized dilemma of wanting comfort and safety from the very same person who is triggering their threat response. Again, the partner may be doing exactly what the couple consented to and acting within their negotiated agreements, but for the pre-existing partner, their primary attachment figure being away, unavailable and potentially sharing levels of intimacy with another person registers as a debilitating threat in the nervous system. As someone in this situation simultaneously wants to move towards and away from one's partner, the very foundation of their relationship and attachment system can begin to shudder, and people can begin acting out in ways that are destructive to each other and the relationship. When this happens, I recommend working with a professional to re-establish inner and outer safety.

CNM can activate the attachment system into primal panic.

From the perspective of attachment theory, we need to be connected to people to survive, so our nervous system equates emotional connection with safety and emotional disconnection with danger or threat. Attachment-related threats include the potential loss of our attachment figure, separation from our attachment figure or loss of access to them for periods of time longer than we are used to. These threats don't have to be actual to activate the attachment system—even theoretical or symbolic threats can initiate attachment distress and what is called primal panic. As Sue Johnson states,

> *Separation distress arises when an attachment*
> *bond is threatened or a secure connection is*
> *lost. There are other kinds of emotional bonds*

> *based on shared activities or respect, and when*
> *they are broken a person may be distressed. But*
> *that distress does not have the same intensity*
> *or significance as when an attachment bond is*
> *called into question. Emotional and physical*
> *isolation from attachment figures is inherently*
> *traumatizing for human beings, beginning*
> *with it as a heightened sense, not simply of*
> *vulnerability and danger, but also helplessness.*[62]

Many of my clients report being highly anxious and off their emotional axis for hours, sometimes even days, before their partner goes on a date with someone else. Others seriously spiral out while the date is happening. Cognitively, they know that their partner is still alive, not abandoning them or doing anything wrong, but their body and emotions are in primal panic. In such cases, jealousy is not a sufficient or accurate description of what is happening for the partner in distress. When primal attachment panic gets mislabeled as jealousy, the partner experiencing it can be left thinking that there is something wrong with them, that this is their issue to figure out on their own and that they should be better at doing CNM. They might use self-destructive behaviors, such as using distractions or substances, in an attempt to feel better, but the root of the problem is left unaddressed. This can also escalate into panic attacks, meltdowns or an emotional crisis that can pit partners against each other or become extremely difficult for everyone involved to manage. However, when people are able to identify this experience as primal panic, understand how it is rooted in their attachment needs, learn how to better self-soothe and address these attachment needs with their partner, a new path forward opens up together.

There can be a mismatch of attachment expectations.

As mentioned earlier, not all relationships have to be attachment-based, but ideally all parties involved in the relationship need to agree about this. Very painful and confusing situations can arise when one person wants a certain relationship to meet their attachment needs, but the other person does not want the same level of involvement, or if a person wants an attachment-based relationship in theory but is practically or situationally unable to emotionally provide at that level. When I see clients struggling with attachment anxiety because a partner gives mixed signals or is inconsistent in their responsiveness, support or availability, it is important to explore whether or not they are expecting this partner to be an attachment figure for them. If they are, then it is paramount for them to dialogue with their partner about whether or not that partner wants to be in the role of an attachment figure for them, as well as honestly assessing if the partner has enough time, capacity and/or space in their life and other relationships to show up to the degree required for being polysecure together.

Some people prefer not to define their relationships, preferring to explore and experience them without labels or traditional expectations. As long as this level of ambiguity or relationship fluidity is a match for everyone involved, it can be a very liberating and satisfying way to relate with others. But when someone casts a partner in the role of attachment figure, but that person is unable or unwilling to play the part, much pain, frustration, disappointment, heartache and attachment anxiety ensues. In monogamy, if two people do not align in their desires to be attached at a secure level or one person is unable or unwilling to step into secure functioning, then the relationship usually ends (or they just suffer miserably together forever), but when this occurs in nonmonogamy, the relationship might also end, but it doesn't necessarily have to. Nonmonogamous relationships allow for more flexibility and negotiation about how close, connected and involved partners want to be. I've seen that once people get clear with each other about whether or not they are pursuing an attachment-based relationship, each person can better orient to what the relationship is, what it isn't, what's available and what's not available, enabling people to better accept and appreciate the relationship for what it is without having to let it go. If the relationship is not going to be attachment-based, this doesn't mean that someone no longer needs to have their attachment needs met in general, but the acceptance that a specific relationship is not going to meet a person's attachment needs can relieve everyone involved and be an important step in finding or creating relationships with others.

Potential signs that your attachment needs are not being considered in your CNM relationship:

- Your partner is inconsistently there for when you need them.
- Your partner ignores your texts, emails or calls or inconsistently responds to your texts, emails or calls.
- Your partner ignores your explicit requests for time together or they keep saying that they want

to do things with you but there is little to no follow-through.

- Your partner does things that make you question if you are accepted, appreciated or valued.
- Your partner is inconsistent about the information they share about themselves, other partners or sexual activity.
- Relationship and/or sexual agreements are being broken.
- Your partner uses their other partners as an excuse for their own behavior.
- Your partner uses criticism, defensiveness, contempt or stonewalling.
- Your feelings, needs or opinions are not heard or don't carry much weight.
- Despite what your partner says about how much they care about you or how they *don't* practice hierarchy, other partners are getting preferential treatment.
- Your partner is effusively affectionate over text, but uncomfortable with verbal or physical affection in person.
- You are giving more than you are receiving.
- You are being asked to keep your relationship a secret or lie about your relationship in front of certain people.
- You get more information from your metamours pertaining to important things about your partner than from your actual partner.

CNM can create new attachment ruptures.

As people transition into the nonmonogamous rela-tionship paradigm they are required to lay down the privileges as well as the relational map of monogamy. Now walking around in a world that does not yet fully understand, respect or approve of them, these people are left to figure out how to ethically have multiple lovers without a clear guidebook to follow. The loss of monogamy's privileges and absence of the clear-cut path that it offers on how to navigate relationships can create new attachment ruptures and traumas, both anticipated and unanticipated. These ruptures can occur over the multiple dimensions of human experience that are presented in the nested model of attachment and trauma. The following section offers the different ways in which people can experience stress, trauma and attachment ruptures when they are practicing nonmonogamy. Some of these experiences are subtler, where difficulty and pain result from an accumulation of stressful experiences within the various levels, and other experiences are more overtly oppressive, traumatic or damaging of attachment. The examples that I share here are based on my own personal and professional experiences with CNM, insights from other mental health professionals specializing in nonmonogamous relationships, and Elisabeth Sheff's years of research on people in polyamorous relationships and families.[63] In Sheff's own words,

> Discrimination is hurtful action taken against an identifiable minority group, and anti-poly discrimination takes many different forms. Using data from my 20-year study of polyamorous families with children, I compiled some of the ways in which polyamorous people report experiencing discrimination. It is important

> *to note that many of the people in the research*
> *reported positive experiences with polyamory,*
> *from family members who fully embraced them,*
> *their partners, and metamours, to friends who*
> *welcomed the new chosen family members*
> *and employers who invited the entire polycule*
> *to the employee holiday dinner. People living*
> *in urban areas, especially in liberal states,*
> *reported less discrimination than people living*
> *in conservative and/or rural regions. Most*
> *respondents were middle-class white people and*
> *did not mention racial or class discrimination,*
> *though respondents of color did mention concern*
> *for polyamory to complicate their already*
> *challenging interactions with racism.*[64]

I have seen firsthand the many ways that being non-monogamous can facilitate positive experiences with the friends, family and work, as well as how many new and unexpected positive experiences people have with partners, metamours and the new friends and family that come about from being nonmonogamous. That said, I've yet to meet someone who is openly nonmonogamous who has not experienced some form of judgment, criticism, rejection, discrimination or othering because of their lifestyle or orientation. Experiences can vary greatly in terms of severity and impact, and the intersectionality of being polyamorous with other forms of marginalization cannot be ignored or minimized. The nested model of attachment and trauma offers a framework to name some of these differences and how they have an effect at each of the different levels.

The Nested Model of Attachment and Trauma Applied to People Practicing CNM

Self Level

People who wake up to themselves as being nonmonogamous as an orientation can have a similar coming-out process as people who come out as gay, lesbian, bisexual or transgender. Even though the realization that someone is nonmonogamous by orientation may come with much personal clarity, relief and alignment of who and how they are, the coming-out process can also bring with it an enormous amount of pain and confusion. Deconstructing monogamy, whether you identify as nonmonogamous by orientation or as a lifestyle choice, is not an easy undoing process for everyone. As people recognize the ways that mono-romantic beliefs have been internalized into their psyche, as well as how these ideas have influenced their actions and choices, regret and shame can arise. The experience can cause a person to question their own identity, uncertain about which elements still fit and which do not, uncertain as to exactly what authenticity and integrity look like for them now. Unable to rely on a sense of self for internal safety and security, these people can be left on shaky ground, often without sufficient support to navigate what can become a crisis of identity, a dark night of the soul or a complete reinvention of the self.

Relationship Level

At the relationship level, trauma and attachment ruptures can arise from:

- Your marriage or relationship disintegrating because you identify as nonmonogamous.

- You and your partner transitioning together to CNM, which you are happy about, but experiencing a real loss of the old relationship that the two of you had together. Even though you might still be together, the relationship has changed, and it's common to have grief about the past relationship with your partner that is no longer, as well as grief and loss about the monogamous future you had envisioned with them.

- Loss, rejection, estrangement, repeated judgment or criticism from friends and family members who you have come out to.

- Being treated differently by friends and family who no longer want you to be around or alone with their spouse or kids because you are nonmonogamous.

- Being subjected to "interventions" from friends and family who are unaccepting of you being nonmonogamous.

- Feeling unsafe and afraid to come out to certain friends or family members because it may end the relationship or risk your future safety or security in some way.

- The loss and stress that can occur from no longer being number one to your partner.

- Breakups or the death of CNM partners, which are just as painful and difficult as breakups or deaths of monogamous partners. Because you have other partners, your friends and family may not recognize or acknowledge the significance of the loss.

- Falling in love with someone who then ends the relationship with you (often suddenly) because

their other partner told them to or they decided
to close up their relationship with their primary partner.

- The loss of metamour relationships when your
  partner and the metamour break up.
- Being unacknowledged, dismissed, stonewalled or
  mistreated by metamours.
- Needing to break up with a partner because they
  choose to stay in a relationship with other people
  who mistreat or abuse them, you, themselves
  or others.
- Partners making a unilateral decision that
  changes the structure of your relationship without
  your consent.
- Being subjected to vetoes or power dynamics from
  partners and/or metamours.
- Not having a say or voice in what things you can do,
  places you can go or sex acts you can experience with
  your partner because of rules and agreements that
  they have with someone else.
- One of your partners enters into a new relationship
  with someone and they get more attention, time,
  access or social recognition than you do.
- Your spouse or primary partner has switched
  to non-hierarchical polyamory or relationship
  anarchy, but you still want to be primary partners
  so you lose the primacy in your relationship that
  you want.
- No longer having your partner as your primary safe
  haven and the person you can tell everything to and
  process everything with.

- Having relationship agreements or safer sex agreements being broken that compromise your health and safety.
- Having to manage your partner's emotional rollercoasters or hurts from the other relationships they are in.

Home Level

At the home level, trauma, discrimination and attachment ruptures can arise from:
- Becoming a target from neighbors, housing associations or landlords because of being nonmonogamous.
- Evictions or denial of housing because you are nonmonogamous.
- The inability to find housing with your partners because of laws that allow only a certain amount of unrelated people to cohabitate.
- Having to navigate and inhabit homes that are built for the married nuclear family.
- Dealing with child custody battles where your children are at risk of being taken out of the home because you are nonmonogamous. Elisabeth Sheff's research has found that most of the child custody court cases that nonmonogamous parents face are *not* initiated by the state or Child Protective Services, but from ex-spouses or the child's grandparents who disapprove of the parent being nonmonogamous.

Culture and Communities Level

At the culture and communities level, trauma, discrimination and attachment ruptures can arise from:

- Being rejected by social groups or communities that you were regularly involved with and previously accepted by.
- Being ostracized from a church that you belong to.
- Being subjected to "interventions" from teachers or community or religious leaders who are unaccepting of nonmonogamy.
- Being unable to bring more than one partner to events, holidays, work functions, graduations or weddings, either because of the potential negative consequences or because of the standard plus-one policy of many formal occasions.
- Already being a part of a minority group that does not fully fit into more mainstream communities and now having to experience even further community discrimination or isolation.
- Being blocked from online groups or being unfriended or unfollowed on social media because of being nonmonogamous.
- Being an outcast at school because of being nonmonogamous.
- Losing your job because you are nonmonogamous.
- Losing your polycule or nonmonogamous community because of drama or a breakup.
- Being unable to be out about being nonmonogamous at work because it could put your job, respect, ranking, promotions, bonuses, clients or social status at risk.
- Being a man (usually white and cisgender) who is facing *not* having certain privileges for the first time.

When nonmonogamous, the loss of monogamous privilege shows up in several of the different levels for everyone, but for men it is usually first noticed in regards to dating, where men practicing CNM no longer have the same ease, accessibility and favor when it comes to dating now that they are nonmonogamous. The transition to CNM can become a significant eye-opener to privilege. While it is extremely important for men (especially white and/ or cisgender men) to face the power dynamics that they have participated in and benefited from, the experience of going through a privilege flip can be disorienting, painful and even traumatic. Men can also experience further ostracization when they are met with contention from nonmonogamous communities because they still hold other forms of privilege, and when they experience a lack of support and guidance in how to make sense of the privileges they've lost and those they still hold.

- Being judged or scolded at the doctor's office for being nonmonogamous.
- Being denied certain STI testing because the doctors or nurses are not aware or accepting of nonmonogamy.
- Being given misinformation about sexual health and STIs from health-care practitioners who have been trained from a mononormative perspective.
- Being denied access to partners who are in the hospital because you are not married.
- No longer seeing yourself in popular culture via songs, commercials, movies, television, news, etc.
- Not being able to find a local nonmonogamous community to participate in.

Societal Level

At the societal level, trauma, discrimination and attachment ruptures can arise from:
- People practicing CNM being a legally unprotected class in the US and most other countries.
- Being unable to legally marry more than one partner.
- Being unable to religiously marry more than one person (this is not true of all religions).
- Nonmonogamy being considered adultery, which is illegal in certain states.
- In the military, nonmonogamy can also be considered adultery, which can put someone's job, ranking and veteran's benefits at risk or even lead to incarceration or being dishonorably discharged from the military.
- Discrimination or the loss of privileges based on the many ways that monogamy and marriage have been institutionalized through tax benefits, health insurance benefits, child rights, estate rights, social security benefits, immigration and citizenship rights and veterans' benefits.

Global Level

At the global level, trauma and attachment ruptures can arise from:
- The collective traumas, deaths and enslavement that the patriarchal, heteronormative and mononormative monogamous paradigms have produced.
- The specific hardships that nonmonogamous people face during a global emergency such as a pandemic. As I write this during the 2020 coronavirus

pandemic, all of my clients, regardless of their relationship structure, are experiencing a maelstrom of fear, overwhelm, anxiety and significant loss. This includes the loss of loved ones, work, home, community, touch, meaning and purpose. However, my nonmonogamous clients are facing additional challenges. Having multiple partners while being asked to practice social distancing and isolation means being separated from important intimate partnerships for an extended period of time. Uncertainty around how long this will go on and concern about the levels of risk that may come with reuniting are also exacerbating their sense of loss, anxiety and overwhelm.

§

When someone is no longer a part of a dominant paradigm, trauma can arise from the experience of being separated from the group and the feeling that they are alone with no one to turn to.[65] Additionally, some experiences specific to being nonmonogamous can create additional and recurring threats that compromise our ability to attach, connect or even function. However, there is much growth that can come from this hardship. Just as scar tissue is stronger than regular skin tissue, traumas can lead to what researchers and mental health professionals refer to as post-traumatic growth, where 30 to 70 percent of individuals who experienced trauma report positive changes arising out of the traumatic experience they went through.[66] Psychologists Richard Tedeschi and Lawrence Calhoun define post-traumatic growth as occurring when "someone's development has surpassed what was present before the struggle with crises occurred. The individual has not only survived, but has experienced changes that are viewed as important, and that go beyond the status quo."[67] Such people have described profound changes in how they view their relationships, as well as how they conceive of themselves and their philosophy of life.

Nonmonogamy can be a pressure cooker for growth. It is commonly and playfully known in the nonmonogamous world that you shouldn't enter CNM unless you are ready to process, communicate, grow and then process, communicate and grow some more. This is because having multiple partners will expose all of your relationship baggage, your blind spots, shadows and shortcomings, and all the potential ways you've been asleep to social issues. Because of this, I've seen how nonmonogamy can actually become an accelerated path to growth, specifically when it comes to attachment, where it offers a path to healing that many people would not experience otherwise. When people are able to heal their previous attachment wounds, address any attachment changes that have occurred since opening up and create relationships that are founded on relational security instead of structural security, what previously felt impossible about CNM becomes possible, even celebratory.

Part *Three*

In this next section we switch to a "how-to" approach to becoming more polysecure. My hope is that almost anyone reading this, monogamous or nonmonogamous, can walk away with concrete ways to further cultivate secure functioning in their relationships. I do the pre-filtering and translating for you so that you don't have to sift, sort through or try to tease apart the monogamous filter that is often applied to attachment literature. Even though attachment exists over the multiple levels of the human experience, this next section focuses on the levels of self and relationship. This is meant to offer you guidance and suggestions, but it is not a substitute for professional support that may be needed for yourself or with your partners.

CHAPTER SEVEN

THE FOUNDATIONS OF BEING POLYSECURE IN YOUR RELATIONSHIPS

UP UNTIL THIS POINT I have predominantly used the umbrella term *nonmonogamy* when talking about people with multiple partners, but as we saw in Chapter Four, people who are nonmonogamous can be quite varied in the ways they practice having multiple partners. As we move further in the discussion of how to be polysecure, I talk specifically about people who are practicing polyamory. Polyamory is commonly defined as being the practice of having romantic love-based relationships with more than one person, and we can add that it is also the form of nonmonogamy where people have multiple romantic attachment figures. As previously mentioned, not all CNM relationships need to be attachment-based. We can have very fulfilling, meaningful, loving and significant relationships with people who we are either less entwined with, don't want to label or define or who we are not looking to actively build an attachment-based relationship with. Ideally, *any* type of relationship, regardless of how involved or not, is ethical, respectful, has open communication and is considerate of everyone involved. But when we are in attachment-based relationships more is required, so the rest of this book will center on people who are (or want to be) in polyamorous attachment-based partnerships.

Do We Want to Be Attachment-Based Partners?

The antecedent to being polysecure with your partners is first getting clear about whether you want to be attachment figures for each other. Our attachment-based relationships take time and investment, and so when referring to attachment-based partners I am referring to a choice that we are making to intentionally cultivate and tend to the attachment-based needs within a particular relationship. Often, falling in love with someone or feeling attached to them does not feel like a choice we make, hence why we call it *falling* in love instead of *stepping* into love. Our attachment figures might be the people we feel levels of connection, compatibility or intensity with right from the start for reasons that we just can't explain, or they may be the people with whom our romantic attachments have organically grown in potency and depth over time. However you come to be with the partners that you already feel attached to or want to cultivate being more polysecure with, what is important is that at some point you are all clear that being attachment-based partners is what you want for the relationship.

In monogamy, usually at some point people have the commitment conversation in hopes of better defining their relationship, but exactly what that means to each person and all of the assumptions and expectations that each person is carrying are often left minimally discussed, if they are articulated at all. In nonmonogamy, unspoken expectations and assumptions typically don't bode very well, and intentional discussions about exactly what we're doing and why we are together are important for everyone involved to feel safe and secure. Since we are talking about attachment-based polyamorous relationships, we are talking about relationships in which you are committed to showing up for each other regularly, prioritizing each other (from choice, not obligation), actively cherishing each other, doing the work required to build a relationship and possibly even building a life together (though having a life commitment is not a prerequisite for secure attachment). Your attachment-based relationships might be with the partners that you refer to as your primary partners, inner circle partners, nesting partners or anchor partners. You may or may not live with them or have children with them, and you definitely do *not* need to do either of those things to be polysecure. People who are solo poly and relationship anarchists can be in securely attached relationships. People who are married and live with their spouse can also have secure attachment–based relationships with their non-nesting partners when vetoes and prescriptive hierarchy are not at play. What matters here is that you have a shared vision about the depth, breadth and level of involvement that you all want together, and that everyone is able to follow through with what you've agreed to.

For us to feel safe and secure in our relationships, we need to know that our partners want to be there for us and will be to the best of their ability, and so some level of commitment to being in a relationship together is important. Depending on what stage of relationship you are in, this might look like:

- A commitment to staying in exploration of the relationship together, without specifically defining the future or integrating your lives.
- A commitment to building an official relationship that you want to have longevity and/or be more interwoven in.
- Commitment to building a life together where you are in it for the long haul.

Commitment can be expressed in many ways. Traditionally it is solidified through marriage, owning property, having kids or wearing certain types of jewelry, but legal, domestic or ornamental undertakings are not the only ways to show dedication. In a 2018 talk on solo polyamory at the Boulder Non-Monogamy Talk Series, Kim Keane offered the following ways that people practicing nonmonogamy can demonstrate commitment to their partners:

- Sharing intimate details (hopes, dreams, fears) and being vulnerable with each other.
- Introducing partners to people who are important to you.
- Helping your partners with moving, packing, homework, job hunting, shopping, etc.
- Having regular time together, both mundane and novel.
- Making the person a priority. (I suggest defining what "being a priority" means to each of you.)
- Planning trips together.
- Being available to partners when they are sick or in need.
- Collaborating on projects together.

- Having frequent communication.
- Offering physical, logistical or emotional support
  (e.g. at doctor's appointments or hospital visits or
  by helping with your partners' family, pets, car,
  children, taxes, etc.).

Commitment Reflection Questions

In each of your relationships that are already attachment-
based, or for the relationships that you would like to
become more attachment-based, discuss the following
questions with your partners:
- What does commitment mean to you?
- What aspects of commitment are most important to
  you (e.g., structural, emotional or public)?
- Why do we want to be attachment figures for
  each other?
- What does being an attachment figure look like
  to you?
- Do we each have the time and availability to offer
  this level of involvement?

The Broad Strokes of Being Polysecure

Once you are clear that being an attachment figure is what
each of you wants, whether in a two-person or multi-
person relationship, figuring out how to do this securely
is the next step. Partners being a safe haven and a secure
base for each other is key for being polysecure.

Being a Safe Haven For Each Other

John Bowlby and his contemporaries believed that for a partner to become an attachment figure, the relationship would serve as both a *safe haven* and a *secure base*.[68] The bedrock of being polysecure in our relationships is feeling that we have a safe haven to turn to. This happens when our partners care about our safety, seek to respond to our distress, help us to co-regulate and soothe and are a source of emotional and physical support and comfort. Similarly, when our partners are struggling or in need, we can be a safe haven by being there for them in warm, caring and receptive ways. When we can't physically be there for our partners, we do as best we can to support them from a distance until we can be in physical proximity.

In search of relationship safety, our attachment system is primed to seek the answers to certain questions regarding our partners. Both consciously and unconsciously we are looking to know:

- If I turn towards you, will you be there for me?
- Will you receive and accept me instead of attack, criticize, dismiss or judge me?
- Will you comfort me?
- Will you respond in a way that calms my nervous system?
- Do I matter to you?
- Do I make a difference in your life?
- Can we lean into and rely on each other?

Interestingly, research consistently shows that people who have safe haven relationships in their life, whether through romantic partnership or through their family, are more resilient in the face of life stressors and trauma. Attachment research has looked at many different populations including orphans, people who have experienced natural disasters, assault victims, veterans who were in combat, refugees, people who were in New York City during 9/11, people in concentration camps in World War II, as well as people who have had heart attacks or are recovering from surgery in the hospital. The research has found that when people in all of these difficult situations have their safe haven attachment figures around them, either during or quickly after the event, they recover faster, experience less physical and emotional pain, and are less likely to have escalating symptoms of PTSD.[69]

Examples of things that you and your partners can do to be safe havens for each other are:

- Give emotional support and comfort.
- Listen to each other with full attention.
- Inquire and share about feelings and needs.
- Track what is going on in each other's lives and make sure to follow up and inquire about those things.
- Help in practical ways when a partner is tired or sick.
- Discuss or debrief events of the day or things that are important to each of you.
- Let your partners know how and why they matter to you.

Safe Haven Reflection Questions

In each of your relationships that are attachment-based or for the relationships that you would like to become more attachment-based, ask yourself:

- How does this partner already act as a safe haven for me?

- In what ways do they show up for me that feel supportive and comforting?
- How can this partner help me feel even more safe with them?
- How can this partner help me feel even more supported or comforted by them, in general or in specific situations?
- In what ways can I show up more as a safe haven for this partner?

Being a Secure Base for Each Other

When safety is established with our attachment figures and we have an internalized felt sense that we can turn towards them and lean on them when needed, we are freed up to securely turn away from them and engage in the world, whether with them by our side or on our own. A secure base provides the platform from which we can move out in the larger world, explore and take risks. This exploration facilitates our sense of personal competence and healthy autonomy. Similar to how children want to show their parents their latest drawings, tricks, accomplishments or discoveries, as adults we need to share the new things we've learned, the things we've achieved and the things we're excited about. Being and having a secure base in our partnerships means supporting each other's personal growth and exploration, independent activities and other relationships, even when these actions require time apart from each other. Secure base partners will not only support our explorations, but will also offer guidance when solicited and lovingly call us on our shit. They function as a compassionate mirror for our blind spots and all the ways we may be fooling ourselves, whether through self-aggrandizement or self-limitation.

While being a secure base may appear to be easier or more fun than being a safe haven, do not underestimate how intimately personal and deeply vulnerable it can be for a person to share their visions, hopes, curiosities and dreams. It also requires faith to be able to turn away from a partner and then trust that you can safely turn back. In simple terms, I see being a safe haven as serving the role of accepting and being with me as I am, and a secure base as supporting me to grow beyond who I am.

Examples of things that you and your partners can do to be secure bases for each other:

- Encourage each other's personal growth and development.
- Support each other's work and/or interests.
- Listen to each other's hopes, dreams and visions.
- Listen when your partners share about their experiences in other relationships (assuming that the information shared is appropriate and consensual).
- Have conversations about things that are intellectually or emotionally stimulating to each other.
- Acknowledge each other's capabilities and possibilities for growth.
- Compassionately bring light to your partner's limitations and blind spots.
- Offer words of encouragement when your partners take on new responsibilities, go on dates with others, take a risk or learn something new.

Secure Base Reflection Questions

In each of your relationships that are attachment-based, or for the relationships that you would like to become more attachment-based, ask yourself:

- How is this partner already acting as a secure base for me?
- What does growth look like for me? Is it usually a shared or a personal experience, or both?
- Are there other ways that I want encouragement or support in my individual growth or with my visions and dreams?
- How could my partners support me in regard to my other relationships?
- How could I better support or encourage my partners' dreams or aspirations to grow and develop?
- How could I better show genuine interest or curiosity in things that are important to my partners?
- How could I better support my partners in their other relationships?

A benefit of nonmonogamy is that you don't have to provide or expect to receive all of this from one partner. Different partners can be more of a safe haven, a secure base or both, offering different facets of each. We all have different strengths and it can be wonderfully satisfying to have some partners that support you in safe haven ways, while others offer more of a secure base.

When I first began presenting at nonmonogamy conferences, I was nervous. I had experience presenting in academic settings and in leading workshops, but the conference format was different. I didn't know whether the nonmonogamous audience would connect with what I was talking about (I was presenting on emotional triggers, so in retrospect it was a slam-dunk topic for nonmonogamous folks). At this time, I was still nursing my infant son on demand, so being away from him for more than three or four hours felt like a big deal. I needed both emotional support and logistical help with my son. Thankfully, I had two different partners who could take on these roles for me.

My co-parent (and husband at the time), Dave, was an amazing secure base. He cleared his day to be with our son and gave me the freedom and encouragement to go rock it as a presenter. He reassured me that my son would be fine while I was gone and that he wouldn't starve if he couldn't nurse at the exact moment he wanted to. Dave reminded me to remember to have fun while I was presenting, which was precisely what I needed to hear right before I gave a talk. In this incident, he was the secure base that I needed to be able to confidently turn away from my family and go take a risk in the larger world. However, since he was caretaking our son, he was understandably not available for any of the safe haven types of emotional support that I also needed. This is where my other partner, Sam, stepped in. Sam wasn't able to be at the conference with me, but they made themself available to talk on the phone right when my talk was done. They were excited to hear about my experience and gave me their full attention as I debriefed everything I needed to. In that instance, Sam was my safe haven. I could let my guard down with them, lean into them, and experience being accepted with love, warmth and attunement. Both partners came through for me exactly how I needed, and neither needed to be or do more than they did.

On a separate but similar note, I presented the information in this chapter at a different polyamorous conference and bumped into an attendee from that conference several months later. She told me that after hearing my talk, she realized that all three of her current partners were a safe haven for her, but that none of them were really functioning in secure base ways. This person was fulfilled and content with how her partners were showing up for her, so she decided not to request that any of them take on more of a secure base role. She also felt that it wasn't necessary to take on a fourth partner who could provide a secure base. Instead, she decided to start acting in more secure base ways for herself, which she did by encouraging her own growth and expansion. In just a few short months she started a blog that she had long thought about and also bought and renovated the vintage car of her dreams. To me, this demonstrates the importance of how we do not always have to turn to our partners to meet our safe haven or secure base needs, especially when our pre-established relationship dynamics are working well. We can focus on cultivating a more secure attachment with ourselves, which is one of the pillars of being polysecure. Chapter Nine focuses on the importance of being our own safe haven and secure base, so that we can better establish a secure attachment with our self. When attachment ruptures and traumas occur, we can lose access to the parts of ourselves that are able to be a safe haven through self-soothing, self-nurturance, self-compassion and self-acceptance, and to the parts of us that are able to be a secure base through self-encouragement, healthy standards, appropriate boundaries and alignment with our values. While having multiple partners to turn to for a secure base or safe haven is a definite benefit of nonmonogamy, we can't forget how powerful and important it is to also rely on our self in these ways.

CHAPTER EIGHT
THE HEARTS OF BEING POLYSECURE

NOW THAT WE'VE COVERED being a safe haven and secure base—the two broader strokes of being polysecure–I want to focus on some more specific things you can do to cultivate being polysecure in your multiple relationships. I've combed through the literature on the conditions needed to create secure attachment in adult romantic relationships and considered what I've experienced and witnessed in the polyamory partnerships that I've counseled. The result is the acronym HEARTS, which I use to encapsulate the different ingredients, skills, capacities and ways of being required for secure functioning in multiple attachment-based partnerships.

H	Here (being here and present with me)
E	Expressed Delight
A	Attunement
R	Rituals and Routines
T	Turning Towards after Conflict
S	Secure Attachment with Self

The first five letters in HEARTS cover the relational level
of being polysecure. When explaining these, I suggest
different behaviors and practices that you can experiment
with and take on in your attachment-based polyamorous
relationships. The S in HEARTS focuses on the individual
level of being polysecure. I have dedicated the whole next
chapter to this, where I will guide you through suggestions
and practices for applying HEART to yourself. An important
caveat is that you do not need to be perfect in all of these
things all of the time, but my hope is that if you prioritize
these things at the heart of your relationships, you will
discover beautiful and powerful ways to thrive in love.

H: Are You Here?

From an infant's perspective, it would be impossible to
attach and bond to someone who is not there. The absence
of caregivers can be dangerous and damaging, and can
have a ripple effect for years to come. Attachment begins
in the body, first in utero and then through skin-to-skin
contact with our caregivers. Physical proximity is needed
for the development of attachment, since it is through
touch and face-to-face contact that we forge bonds with
each other, and it is by responding to a child's cries with
our own bodies that we inform them that they are safe
and not alone. Voice also plays an important role in the
attachment system.* The right tone and cadence from

---

* Since voice is so important to attachment, I don't want to
dismiss that there are people who have never met in person,
but do fall in love or start to feel intense attachments to each

our attachment figures can have the powerful ability to soothe us when distressed, and a person's voice and body language can also alert us to how trusting and safe they are.

Optimal functioning of the attachment system and the formation of attachment security are best facilitated by consistent interactions with significant others who are responsive to our needs for proximity. We need to know that our attachment figures are available to us, that they are within arm's reach (literally and virtually) and that they will be available and responsive when we call for them. When we experience our partners as being *here with us*, it results in the positive beliefs that our partners care about us, we matter to them and we are worthy of their love and attention. Conversely, when our partners are unavailable, unresponsive or mentally elsewhere, attachment insecurity can arise, feeding the fears and doubts that we are not valued, loved or worthy.

The Buddhist monk and peace activist Thich Nhat Hanh is widely attributed as providing the quote "the most precious gift we can offer is our presence," but entrepreneur Malcolm Forbes is said to have reminded us that "presence is more than just being there." Being in the same physical space does not necessarily mean that you are here and present with the people you are near.

---

other just by talking on the phone or even messaging. However, I would put those experiences into the category of new relationship energy, limerence or possibly idealization, rather than include them in the formation of actual secure attachment.

When you are with your partners, are you really focusing on them and giving your full attention, or are you distracted by your phone, by the stresses from the day, by your worries about the future or by your other partners? Are you really listening to your partners when they talk, or are you thinking about other things, only partially listening or mentally preparing for what you want to say next? Physical proximity is extremely important and necessary for attachment, but it is not sufficient if the quality of presence is poor. Being present with your partner is important for people in any relationship structure, but struggling with presence and availability is a common complaint in nonmonogamous relationships since there are typically more people to attend to in any given day or week. One of the most common complaints that I hear is of situations where partners are spending quality time together and one partner is messaging with other people in ways that feel distracting and interruptive.

Attachment is an embodied experience, and it is first through being present with ourselves in our own bodies and present with our loved ones that the rest of the attachment-based skills and capacities of the HEART of being polysecure can be developed and expressed. As an adult who wants to function from a secure place in your relationships, you can't affirm, attune, repair or even play if you are not *here* with yourself or with your partners. Being present is not just putting your phone down for a few minutes. It is a way of being, from interaction to interaction, where you consciously inhabit your own body and show up with the best of your attention, offering your presence as a gift.

Questions to Consider

- How do you show that you are here with your partners?
- How could you be more present when you are with your partners?
- Are there ways that you could be more available and responsive to your partners?
- How do your partners demonstrate that they are being present with you?
- Do you trust that your partners will be available and responsive if and when you need them?
- Are there things that your partners could do that would enhance your sense that they are here with you when you are together and here for you in general?

Things to Try and to Experiment With

- In order to be truly present with one another, we need to experience and have access to an inner state that is different from our ordinary state of consciousness. To do this, it is important to learn practices that cultivate a state of presence so that you can bring this to the people you are with. Explore different practices to create a state of presence and mindfulness.
- Articulate being here and present as a value that you have for yourself and as an intention in your relationships.
- Prioritize regular time with your partners when you are both fully here and present with each other. This is especially important when you only get limited time together, but it is just as important when you live together and spend a lot of time in each other's

company, but are not actually connecting without
the distractions of kids, house, work, pets, meals, etc.

- Put your phone down, take your smartwatch off. If
you are on a date with a partner, put your electronic
devices away. With the exceptions of legitimate
situations that need urgent and immediate attention,
do your best to take care of any messaging, logistics
or calls with other partners before or after your date.
If you have partners who can't handle not being in
contact with you for a period of time, professional
support might be needed to work through attachment insecurities or patterns of codependency. Even
though attachment-based relationships do require
regular maintenance, when we are functioning from
secure attachment with our partners we will be
flexible, gracious, tolerant and even appreciative of
time apart.

- There will be times when having your phone away
is not realistic. For example, if you nest with your
partner and you are both home together, but it's not
necessarily designated quality time together, or if
you and a partner are on an extended trip and it's
not realistic to not talk to other partners for several
days. In these situations, I find that it is best to just
be transparent about when you need to step away
and message or make calls. Do your best not to sneak
in messages to others while the partners you are
with are in the bathroom or while you're lying in bed
together (unless your partners truly take no offense
at this, which some people don't). With nesting
partners, it can be helpful to have designated times
of the day or during the week where you are both off
your phone and focused on each other, so that the

times when you are on your phone throughout the day do not become problematic. When you are with non-nesting partners, clearly let them know when you need a certain amount of time to be on your phone and that you'll be fully present when you're back. This can go a long way in preventing tensions and strain.

- When you are struggling with being present because you are in conflict with another partner or have other life stressors going on, the next best thing you can do is to just name what is tugging at your presence. You do not necessarily have to go fully into what is distracting you since you might not want to spend your time with one partner processing what's going on with another, and some of the things that you are struggling with may require honoring the privacy of your other partners, but being able to name where you are at and what is preventing you from being fully present (instead of trying to pretend that you're fine when you're clearly not) is another way of being present with where you are in that moment. It may not be ideal, but it is honest and partners will typically appreciate this.

- In your relationships, discuss how available you want to be to each other (i.e., to what extent or at what frequency), be clear about what you can generally offer and follow through regarding time, attention and forms of communication.

- As best as you can, clearly communicate when you will be unavailable, whether that is times during the day, specific days of the week, standing dates with certain partners, trips, holidays, etc. When we can't be available to our partners, the next best thing for both of our attachment systems is to tell them when we will be out of reach and when we will be back. If you can't be immediately available to one of your partners, the next best thing you can do is let them know when you can, so that they know what to expect.

E: Expressed Delight

The next thing that you can do to nurture more polysecurity with your partners is offer *expressed delight*. Brown and Elliot describe expressed delight as one of the foundational elements of secure attachment.[70] When a parent shows pleasure not just in the things that their child does, but in who their child *is*, a positive sense of self and healthy self-esteem are fostered in the child. As adults, expressed delight is also needed to promote secure attachment and a healthy sense of self within the relationship. When our partners are able to articulate the ways that we are special and valuable to them, our interpersonal self-worth is supported. When we express the ways that we appreciate and are grateful for our partners, we create a culture of positivity in our relationships that allows mutual vulnerability, authenticity and joy to flourish. We can express the delight we have for our partners through our words, our actions, our touch, as well as just the look in our eyes. Diane Poole Heller and her colleagues use the term *beam gleam* (also known as the attachment gaze) to refer to the nonverbal expression of warmth, kindness and love that radiates from our eyes, letting our partners know that they are special to us.

In nonmonogamy, expressed delight is imperative. The paradigm shift from the monogamous mindset of *I am with you because you are the only one for me* to the nonmonogamous view that *I am with you because you are special and unique, but not the only one*, can be difficult to grasp. Even when people don't want to be, the hangover of monogamous thinking often leaves people feeling competitive with their metamours and/or doubtful as to why their partners would want to be with them if they don't have the specific qualities, circumstances, sexual interests or physical attributes that other partners have. Even when people have a healthy sense of self and esteem, they still need positive feedback as to why their partners cherish them and choose to be with them, especially when, theoretically, they can choose to be with many others. There is nothing wrong with needing to hear why you are wanted and valued by your partners and it is important for you to be able to communicate to your partners why they specifically matter to you. Experiencing expressed delight and knowing the ways you are precious in your partners' lives can be an important resource to lean on when feeling jealous or threatened by a metamour or potential new partners. Instead of spinning out into doubt and fear, being able to recall the ways your partners experience you as special, even irreplaceable, can soothe the anxious mind and allow for more compersion to arise.

Questions to Consider
- How do you already show expressed delight for your partners?
- Would your partners like more or different expressed delight from you? How can you provide this?

- How do your partners let you know that you are unique, special and precious to them?
- Are there additional or different ways that you would like to experience expressed delight from your partners?
- Are there certain situations (e.g., before or after your partner is out on a date with someone else) that expressed delight is more or less supportive to you and/or your partners?

Things to Try and to Experiment With

- Let your partner know in spoken and/or written word how they enrich your life.
- Let your partner know in spoken and/or written word how unique and special they are to you.
- Let your partner know in spoken and/or written word the specific things that you love and appreciate about them. These should be based on who they *are* versus the things that they do for you.
- If you are less of a verbal type, make a meal, do a dance, create a piece of art or do something fitting to your style that is effective at intentionally representing and expressing to your partners how unique and precious they are to you.
- After spending time with a partner, let them know the things you enjoyed about your time together and what specific things they did that were meaningful to you. You can do this either right when you are saying goodbye, as you are going to bed together or within a few hours or days after you were together.
- With your partners, take on a gratitude practice where you set aside a regular time to each appreciate the ways in which they've been supportive or shown

up that have been meaningful to each of you. You
can share something your partner did that you
are grateful for at the end of each day, or you can
set aside a few minutes once a week to share your
gratitude from the week.

- Flash your partner the eyes! You'd be surprised
what just three seconds of the attachment gaze/
beam gleam can do to fortify your attachment
bond. When in a new relationship with someone,
we rarely have to remind ourselves of this because
everything in our body is easily oozing that this
person is the eighth wonder of the world to us, but
bringing this back in our longer-term relationships
can support feeling that spark again. Seeing our
partners giving the attachment gaze to other people
might be painful when we are no longer in new relationship energy with that partner. Try intentionally
sending the beam gleam to your partners and you
will be pleasantly surprised at what it can do to feed
each other's attachment systems and strengthen
your connection.

A: Attunement

Our attachment bonds are emotional bonds, and being
able to emotionally tune into and connect with our partners is at the core of feeling safe and secure together.
Attunement is a state of resonance with our partners and
the act of turning towards them in an attempt to understand the fullness of their perspective and experience.
Attuning to a partner does not mean that you have to
agree with them and take on their experience as your

own, but it does mean that you are willing to join them in their internal emotional world and their inner state of mind in order to empathize with what they are going through. Attunement is meeting your partner with curiosity, wanting to understand their feelings and needs. It is the feeling of being seen, understood and "gotten" by the other. As children, it is through being attuned to by our attachment figures, by having them mirror and match our experiences and help us make sense of our inner experiences, that we are able to then develop the ability to identify our own thoughts and emotions and subsequently self-regulate these emotional and mental states. As adults we still need to be met and understood in order to best regulate ourselves. It is through being connected with others, and through feeling held, understood and supported by others that we are able to tolerate and regulate our own emotional responses.

There are certain challenges with attunement that can surface in attachment-based relationships. They include how to stay attuned to your partner when they are upset with you and how to stay attuned if you get triggered by them. In nonmonogamous relationships it can be additionally challenging to stay attuned to your partner when they are talking about one of their other partners, when jealousy arises or when the things they are sharing about others have implications for your relationship with them. When you are with multiple partners at the same time, you might also feel confusion around how to stay attuned to each of your partners. Just as the wants and needs of each relationship are different, the ways that we attune to each of our partners can also be different.

Questions to Consider
- How do you experience your partners as attuning to you?
- How do you know that your partners "get" you and care about your experience?
- In what ways do you already attune to your partners?
- How could you better or differently attune to your partners to support them in feeling even more seen and understood?
- Are there ways that you would like your partners to better or differently attune to you that would support you in feeling even more seen and understood?

Things to Try and to Experiment With
- Listen with your heart. When listening to your partner, put your solution-orientated brain aside for a few minutes. Soften your eyes, bring warmth to your face, open up your heart and listen.
- Ask questions from genuine curiosity and the desire to truly understand, rather than from preconceived notions about what your partner has already done or what you think they should do. Be careful about asking questions that are really just searching for evidence to either make yourself feel better, to prove them wrong or to expose them as lying in some way. Also, be careful not to interrogate or manipulate through your questions.
- Make an effort to track something that your partner is going through. For example, if you know they went to an event or have an aunt in the hospital, follow up by asking them how the event was or how their aunt is doing.

- Genuinely ask your partner about how they are doing, whether in general or about something specific. Use open-ended questions that encourage them to share any feelings or needs they have surrounding the situation, what their experience has been, what it means to them and how they have been impacted by it.

- Bring your bodies into attunement. Sex can be a great way to do this, especially if you take turns just focusing on what one partner likes and wants. You can also explore techniques and exercises such as sitting or spooning and breathing together, bringing your bodies and breath into harmony in nonsexual ways.

- Take a pause in your day, think about something that you know one of your partners is grappling with and put yourself in their shoes for a few minutes.

- When listening to your partner talk about another partner (or something else that has the potential to trigger you) put your friend hat on instead of your partner hat. Any concerns or questions that you may have can still be brought up eventually, but do your best to initially separate what they are sharing and what it means to them from how it impacts you.

- Slow down your conversation by taking turns paraphrasing what you just heard the other partner say before you respond to what they said.

- Learn non-violent communication or other empathy-based techniques that encourage you to empathically reflect back to your partner what they are feeling and needing.

- Check out John Gottman's book *The Science of Trust: Emotional Attunement for Couples.*

R: Rituals and Routines

Our attachment system is comforted by routine and regularity. In our relationships with our attachment figures, we tend to prefer partners who are more reliable and situations where we can experience the ease of generally knowing what to expect and not be surprised to the point of disruption. The mundane rituals of everyday life can put many of our worries to rest and remind us that we are an integral part of our partners' lives, and the profound rituals of commitment ceremonies and rites of passage can significantly deepen and strengthen our bonds. The outer commitment we make to a relationship through ceremonies or officially asking someone to be our partner can offer structure and definition, and the day-to-day ways that we engage with one another—the micro routines and rituals of relationship that we create—can be seen as the inner commitment we make to show up for the relationship wholeheartedly and not just because there might be an outer, more explicit commitment to rely on.

In monogamy, the daily routines of a relationship can be easier to fall into. There are only two people to consider, and the larger rituals and relationship rites of passage such as marriage, having children or moving in together are more obvious, culturally expected and supported. In nonmonogamy, socially recognized ways of honoring the relationship can be less clear, and it can be more difficult to find our rhythm with a partner, especially when we don't live with our partner and/or when one of you already lives with other partners. Nonmonogamous relationships do have their own relationship rites of passage, like first sleepovers, trips away together or having sex without a barrier for the first time, but the significance of these events can be easily missed by normative standards. However, it is just as important in our nonmonogamous relationships to find the special things, big and small, that we do with our partners. The routines that we can rely on and look forward to are an important part of secure functioning in our CNM attachment-based relationships.

It is also important to create rituals and routines that honor the transitional moments when you and your partners are parting or reuniting. Our attachment systems are very sensitive to comings and goings. Abrupt departures and sudden arrivals can all be jarring to the nervous system, and hellos or goodbyes left unacknowledged can be disconnective. Understanding what we need to reconnect after being apart from our partner and what we might need to feel secure when saying goodbye might seem like subtle things to focus on, but they should not be underestimated in their impact. One polyamorous colleague of mine intentionally knows the love languages† of each of his different partners, and when they reunite after being apart he does his best to immediately give them their primary love language as a way to reinforce their connection and set the stage for the rest of their time together.

---

† The five love languages, developed by Gary Chapman, are Acts of Service, Quality Time, Words of Affirmation, Physical Touch and Receiving Gifts.

Additionally, how partners say goodbye before one of them goes on a date with someone else or how they reunite after having been with other partners can make a big difference in feeling safe and sound with each other. Some people don't want much pomp and circumstance when saying goodbye, while others need moments of connection with each other before their partner goes off on a date with someone else. If partners live together, they may request that the partner who has been with someone else shower before coming to bed, they may desire emotional or physical contact after being apart or they may prefer to sleep in separate rooms on date nights with others.

While having routines is definitely important in our attachment-based relationships, having times where we also break out of our routines can be just as significant. We can easily fall into default patterns and ruts in our relationships. Remembering the importance of stepping out of our day-to-day cycles, focusing on some novelty, play and adventure can revivify and strengthen our connections with partners.

Questions to Consider
- What are the routines my partners and I already have that are meaningful to me and support me in feeling safe and secure together?
- What rituals have we participated in or what relationship rites of passage have we gone through that have brought us closer?
- How do I like to be celebrated or to celebrate others?
- Are there any daily or regular routines that would support me in feeling more secure with my partners?
- Are there any relationship rites of passage or rituals that could further deepen our bond?

- What do you and your partners each need to reconnect with each other after being apart?
- Are there ways of checking in or saying goodbye before going on a date with another person that would create more safety and security? How do you want to connect or be approached afterwards?

Things to Try and to Experiment With
- Create bedtime or waking rituals with your partners, whether or not you live together. Make sure to also support and allow space for your nesting partners to create their own bedtime and waking rituals with other partners.
- Celebrate birthdays, anniversaries and accomplishments with your partners. When it comes to birthdays, communicate ahead of time about what your hopes and desires are for your birthday and be careful about expecting your partner to be with *you* on *their* birthday just because that's what you would prefer. Give your partners the autonomy to spend their birthday however and with whomever they would like. It's not your day to claim.
- Grieve losses and transitions together.
- Create holiday rituals that honor the relationship, whether or not they are on the actual day of the holiday.
- Create standing dates and dedicate time to regular activities together. Be transparent with partners about any standing dates you already have with other partners or any standing dates that you are looking to create. Also, be transparent with your partners about specific activities or terms of endearment that are designated just for certain

relationships. Some polyamorous people believe that you should never have certain things or places that only belong to one relationship, while other people have few qualms about this. I take the middle path on this issue because I don't know if it is completely realistic to abolish all expressions of "what's ours" from a relationship (some forms of couple identity can be very healthy in polyamory) and I've also seen the powerful healing effect that can happen when people are allowed to ask for something they want to stay within a certain relationship. As long as it's transparent and understood to everyone involved what things belong to a certain relationship and why, it can work well. It is additionally important that all relationships have the freedom to be able to organically create their own version of the things or activities that are theirs. It's key that requests are reasonable (e.g., we like to listen to this specific podcast together or please call only me "sugar puff" rather than limits such as you can't go to Mexico with anyone else or you can only do this sexual position with me). Allocating certain things to relationships can be workable, but definitely tread carefully and transparently, because these waters can become dangerous and hierarchical very quickly.

- Create pet names and special terms of endearment for each other. It's OK to ask that some names or terms of endearment are only shared with each other. But again, be reasonable and very conscious and inclusive of as many partners as possible when setting up such agreements.
- Have a commitment ceremony with your partner. Currently in the United States, people can only get

legally married to one person at a time, but there is nothing that stops you from having commitment ceremonies with other partners. You can create your own ceremony that you conduct together, you can have friends, family members, mentors or other partners officiate a ceremony for you, or you can find an officiant friendly to nonmonogamy to help you co-create and perform a ceremony that is meaningful to you and your partners.

- Step *out* of your routines and rituals. Set aside a day that is unscheduled to spend together, whether at home or doing something out in the world that you normally don't do together.

T: Turning Towards after Conflict

In any relationship, ruptures are inevitable. Relationships are not static but an ongoing flow of harmony to disharmony, rupture and repair, connection, disconnection and back into connection again. We are all different from each other and so we are all eventually going to slip up, make mistakes, say things that we wish we could take back or forget things that are important to our partners. Even if we wanted to be, we can't be perfectly present and attentive to our partners all the time, every time. What matters is not that we have ruptures, but how we repair them. When there is conflict and disagreement or when attunement and connection have been lost, it is how we repair and find our way back to our partners that builds secure attachment and relational resilience. Conflicts left unrepaired can leave lasting effects on our sense of trust, safety and security. In terms of attachment styles, people functioning from a secure style are more likely to use constructive and mutually beneficial problem-solving strategies than people who are more anxiously attached. They are also more likely to accommodate their partners than people who are avoidantly attached, demonstrating their joint concern for their own interests and their partner's interests as well as for enhancing the relationship.

The Gottman Institute has conducted decades of research on couples and found that the main difference between happy couples and unhappy couples is not that happy couples don't have arguments or make mistakes, but that they are better and faster at doing the repair work when breaches have occurred.[71] Couples that are described as the *masters* of relationships, versus what the Gottman Institute names the *disasters* of relationships, still experience episodes of yelling, being mean to each other, defensiveness, being critical or shutting down, but these couples are also willing to admit responsibility for their part in the conflict so they can begin the process of healing their bond. The masters of relationships are able to learn from what went wrong and see that repairing the relationship is more important than the problem itself. The Gottman Institute also found that how skillful someone's repair attempt was did not necessarily predict how effective the repair was. Repairs didn't have to be perfectly executed as much as they had to be genuine. I often tell couples and multiple-partner relationships that you can have all the communication techniques and conflict resolution skills in the world, but they do nothing if you still have an attitude of wanting to either be right or prove your partner wrong. I still recommend acquiring more communication and conflict resolution skills, but even without these, the right attitude—one of repair responsibility, humility and openness—goes far.

The Gottman Institute also found that resilience after conflict was related to how much a couple was making regular "deposits into their emotional bank account." Repair attempts are much more successful when there is a pre-existing relationship culture of understanding each other, expressing gratitude and regularly doing nice things for each other, which supports the relationship in being better able to withstand the inevitable storms. Relationships that are regularly distant or disrespectful have much less success with their repair attempts, no matter how beautiful the attempt is. If you are already doing the HEAR of the HEARTS of secure functioning, you will find that conflict may still arise, but the repair work goes much more smoothly and even brings you closer together in the end.

Questions to Consider
- Are there certain themes to the conflicts that you have with your partners?
- When there has been a rupture, do you and your partners already repair well? How do you do this?
- How are you at offering a repair? What comes easily to you and what feels difficult?
- How are you with receiving a repair from your partners?
- When there has been a rupture, what things could you do differently to better repair with your partner? What requests do you have for your partners around this?

Things to Try and to Experiment With

- If a conflict begins over text, pause until you can either get face-to-face with each other or voice-to-voice, which will help in preventing further misunderstandings and spiraling out.

- Don't be afraid to take a time-out if things get too heated. Many people know that taking a breather when conflict is high would probably be a good idea, but they keep trying to talk or process anyway, even though it is getting them nowhere or already getting nasty. When disagreements and conflict escalate to a point where you feel stuck, when you are triggered, or when there is name-calling, criticism or blaming, take a pause. Just make sure not to walk away without saying anything to your partners. Instead, let them know that you need to cool off and together decide when you'll come back together to address the issues at hand. What I'm describing here is the difference between a reactionary or habitual fleeing and withdrawing, which can be counterproductive, and consciously taking a breather, which can be very productive when conflicts get too hot.

- Keep your desire to be right in check. Remember your desire to be in the relationship and as best as you can, try to stay rooted in being respectful to yourself and your partners, not just one or the other.

- Check out the *The Five Languages of Apology*, by Gary Chapman.

- If you experience regular conflict with a partner (or maybe it's less frequent conflict but very destabilizing when it arises), when *not* in conflict have a conversation about what each of you needs,

> where you see sticky points that can be avoided or
> mitigated and what each of you needs for repair.

- Seek the support of a third party if conflicts are
  recurrent or seem unsolvable.
- Check out the R.A.D.A.R relationship check-in
  method as developed by the Multiamory podcast
  crew to support regular check-ins and conflict management.

§

In this chapter, we explored how to cultivate polysecurity in your multiple attachment-based relationships.
Implementing the suggestions in this chapter could take
months or even years. Because of this, I suggest that you
start where you are. In an ideal setup, you would take a
certain amount of time to focus on each letter in HEART
(e.g., two weeks on being here with your partners and
then two weeks on expressed delight, and so on), so that
you can really dive in and get the lived experience of what
each of these components feels like and looks like. You
may find that you already do some of these letters really
well but other letters, not so much. You can skip around
based on the needs of your particular relationship, but
I would not recommend skipping over a letter entirely.
Each one relates to and builds upon the previous in
ways that are important for you and your partners to be
polysecure. Some of you may also need to begin with the
next chapter, on creating secure attachment with yourself
before you are ready to apply the HEART of polysecurity in
a relationship.

CHAPTER NINE
THE S IN HEARTS—SECURE ATTACHMENT WITH SELF

IT IS TREMENDOUSLY IMPORTANT to have relationships with partners where you are able to put into practice the HEART of being polysecure. Being seen, understood, appreciated and loved by another who is turning towards you with their presence and warmth is invaluable in its potential to offer the corrective attachment experiences that so many of us need. But healing attachment does not stop there. While I will not diminish the power that secure relationships with others have to heal our past and to bring alive our own secure ways, the establishment of a secure relationship with our self is needed to fully embody healthy attachment with others, so much so that it requires its own chapter.

When we have experienced attachment insecurity with caregivers—whether in childhood, in our adult relationships or as disruptions in any of the levels discussed in the nested model of attachment and trauma—our primary relationship with our self can become severed and the development of certain capacities and skills can become compromised. Attachment ruptures and trauma can also leave lasting marks on our psyche, distorting our sense of self through the beliefs that we do not matter, that we are flawed, broken, unworthy or too much while, simultaneously, not enough. This is what needs to be repaired, and in many ways it is the only aspect of our healing that we are truly in control of, since the HEART of being polysecure requires partners to practice with and the other levels require group- or collective-based processes that typically go beyond the individual level.

Internal attachment healing is needed for the HEART of secure functioning to become possible and then take root in our relationships. Even in the most remarkably secure relationships, being together forever is not a given. Your lives might still take you in different directions, partners can die, and even when partners are actively involved with you it is unrealistic to expect them to be there for you every time you are in need. When we are relating from attachment insecurity we can easily (and often unconsciously) put too much onto our partners. We can make our partners into the source of our hope, love, strength, ability to feel or regulate our own emotions, as well as the source of our meaning and purpose in life. Our partners can be the inspiration for these things, as well as the objects or focus of our love, but they should not be the source of it. *You* are the source of your happiness, love, courage, emotional regulation and purpose, and the sooner that you can release your partner from being the source of these experiences the better for everyone involved (metamours included).

Knowing how to stand securely on your own two feet and how to be your own safe haven and secure base is fundamental to building your internal secure attachment.

I would say this to anyone practicing monogamy, but it is even more imperative in nonmonogamous relationships. In polyamory, we need the internal security of being anchored in our inner strength and inner nurturer to navigate a relationship structure that is considerably less secure. Inner security is also imperative because depending on a certain partner as our only go-to support system regarding our relationship with another partner, a shared partner or one of their partners can be triangulating, messy, inappropriate, divisive and even damaging. You must be a priority in your own life. Secure attachment with yourself means being aware of your feelings and desires, as well as being able to tend to your own needs and knowing how to advocate for them in relationships. In the absence of this, your relationships can be built upon a false premise, or, at the very least, will struggle to be sustainable.

Earned Secure Attachment

Those of us who did not experience a securely attached childhood or who have had significant attachment insecurity from our adult relationships can still develop *earned secure attachment*. Meaningful contact with teachers, friends, lovers, mentors, therapists, or other relatives who can empathically resonate and securely bond with us can all assist us in adjusting our attachment style towards becoming more secure. At the self level, one way to develop earned secure attachment is through making sense of your story.

According to Daniel Siegel, we can make sense of our attachment history by creating a coherent narrative of our past experiences.[72] We do this by putting together the story of what we went through as a child and examining how our attachment history impacts our present sense of self and our relationships today. By telling the stories that have been previously unspoken, we allow ourselves to feel what has been unfelt and bring love to what has seemed unlovable. When we are able to describe our painful past experiences and craft them into a narrative that makes sense to us, healing occurs and our brains can literally be rewired for more secure functioning. Daniel Siegel's research has also shown that the main predictor of a child's attachment style is not whether or not their parents had an insecure or secure attachment style, but whether or not their parents were able to make sense of their own attachment history. When parents had trauma and attachment insecurity but were able to create a coherent narrative of what they went through, they were then able to break the cycle of attachment insecurity that can easily get passed down from one generation to the next and, instead, parent their own child from an earned secure stance. As adults, when we experience relationship traumas, painful breakups or losses, creating a coherent narrative about what happened is just as indispensable for our healing and integration.

Nonmonogamy can feature certain kinds of loss and breakups that don't happen anywhere else in our culture. In discussing why or how a relationship ended, we may not have the same common language that is used in describing monogamous endings, or encounter the same level of acceptance and understanding. You may have more partners who could support you post-breakup, and many people definitely benefit from this, but I also see people who feel even more isolated and alone when their nonmonogamous relationship ends. Current partners may get tired of hearing about pain or drama from the relationship that ended, for instance, or it may be inappropriate to process the breakup with current partners (perhaps they are involved with the partner you broke up with). You may also simply not have relationships that you would turn to for this kind of emotional support. The loss of relationships with metamours or entire polycules that result from a breakup can also be confusing, disorienting and painful beyond measure. All of this can leave people feeling as if they are floating in outer space with no sense of what's up and what's down, nothing to ground them and help them move forward. In such cases, finding coherence to your story can be a profound support.

When crafting the stories of your insecurely attached past, it is important not only to be able to describe and allow the feelings associated with what you've gone through, but to also develop an appreciation for the attachment survival adaptations that you took on. Our attachment styles are a result of our response to how available connection was to us. When connection is unavailable, inconsistent, intrusive, dangerous or out of reach, the attachment system will either start to hyperactivate or deactivate as a survival strategy. Your attachment adaptations are what worked best in the environment that you were embedded in, and it is important to recognize the power and wisdom in the different styles that you constructed. As we give voice to our past, accept and allow our pain and even appreciate the ways we were shaped from this, we are better able to take responsibility for the ways that we still need to grow and show up differently for ourselves and in our relationships. We no longer have to be victims of our past, but can be victorious in the face of it.

Go HEART Yourself

The HEART of secure functioning is not just for your relationships with partners, but can be directly applied to your relationship with yourself.

H: Being Here with Myself

In order to create internal security, we must first inhabit our own being. We must fully occupy our bodies, which are the storehouse of our feelings, needs, pains, desires and longings. When there has been attachment insecurity or trauma, being in your body may not be safe or easy, especially when habits of defensiveness, dissociation or disconnection have been at play for years or decades. Traumas can limit our ability for presence. When we detach from ourselves, whether through pulling too far into ourselves or jumping too far out of ourselves into another, we lose access to our own internal states and therefore our own internal resources. We are not truly here in the moment, whether with ourselves or another.

Being our own safe haven and secure base requires that we first have the capacity to be with our self. To sit, to listen, to be available to whatever arises within us. Life occurs in the present moment and our healing needs the fullness of our attention in the here and now to take place. Through embodiment, we can learn how to tolerate the uncomfortable feelings and sensations that might be necessary to move through in order to heal. We can also learn to allow positive sensations and feelings that might have been previously exiled.

Questions to Consider

- In general, how comfortable or uncomfortable do you feel being alone with yourself?
- What are the subtle and overt ways that you avoid being present with yourself?
- What does being present with yourself mean to you? How would it look?
- What does being more embodied mean to you? How would that look?
- If you were more present and embodied, what possibilities in your life or relationship could open up?

Things to Try and to Experiment With

- Mindfulness techniques and meditation practices.
- Body awareness practices (e.g., yoga, dance, walking meditation, body scan meditations).
- Breathwork.
- Emotional or energetic grounding techniques.
- Working with a somatic practitioner or body-based psychotherapist.
- Taking a walk or drive without making calls or listening to anything.
- Sitting with yourself quietly and allowing yourself to be with whatever arises.
- Singing or chanting when you're by yourself without worrying about how you sound.

E: Expressed Delight for Myself

When applying the attachment need of expressed delight to yourself, we are talking about an inner sense of joy, appreciation and pleasure in your own being and existence. As children, it is through mirroring, reflection and the expressed delight from our attachment figures that we are able to develop a positive sense of self and learn what we are capable of. As adults, we still need this and will typically get this through our closest relationships. When another is able to mirror us and take delight in who we are, we can get to know ourselves even more than we did before. But as adults, our positive sense of self cannot be solely contingent on the expressed delight of those around us. We need to cultivate expressed delight for ourselves in order to maintain a positive sense of worth and healthy appreciation for who and how we are that is sustainable and resilient.

Imagine making a mistake and your response to yourself is one of understanding and forgiveness. Imagine looking in the mirror and having thoughts of acceptance and self-compassion. Imagine looking forward to having some solo time because you enjoy time with yourself and are even pleasantly entertained with who you are. For those of you having flashbacks of the *Saturday Night Live* comedy skit where the character Stuart Smalley looks adoringly in the mirror at himself as he says, "I'm good enough, I'm smart enough, and doggone it, people like me," don't worry—I won't suggest looking in the mirror as you say positive affirmations to yourself. I am talking about the importance of positive self-talk and being kind and loving to yourself in ways that you would probably treat a friend, but so frequently forget when it comes to your relationship with yourself. When we have experienced trauma and attachment ruptures, we can forget what it means to be kind to ourselves.

Even a small shift in the way you talk to yourself has significant physical and mental health benefits and can influence your ability to regulate your feelings, thoughts, and behavior under stress. Positive self-talk is not about placating yourself, trying to falsely boost your ego or being self-delusional. It is about having an inner dialogue that is forgiving, understanding, flexible and holds a larger, often more realistic, perspective than the negative, defeated or abusive self-talk that we often tolerate as the inner status quo. Expressed delight for yourself would mean being able to see your strengths, positive attributes, qualities and ways of being that you can be proud of and grateful for, as well as seeing where there is still room for self-improvement. When we delight in our children or our partners, we don't necessarily see them as perfect. In fact, we usually see them with all their amazing, difficult and quirky qualities and choose to take delight in their full-ness, contradictions and all. Can you do this for yourself?

I see the inner critic and shame as the largest obsta-cles to rewiring our inner narratives to reflect more self-expressed delight. Trauma and insecure attachment give birth to our inner critic and shame, and, just as positive self-talk has health benefits, negative self-talk can have far-reaching negative impacts on our health and can actually activate our threat system, spiraling us into the fight/flight/freeze/appease response, just from our own thinking. It is difficult to embody self-worth when we have parts of ourselves that incessantly beat us up for what we've done, what we haven't done, or how we look. The inner critic is the voice in our head that is harsh, mean, critical, unsympathetic, punishing, shaming and "shoulding." Shame is the part of us that feels beat up by the inner critic, accepting what it says as true and believing that we are unworthy, not enough, too much, fundamentally broken and maybe even better off dead.

Shame researcher Brené Brown makes the important distinction between guilt and shame, with guilt being the perspective that *I've done something wrong*, which can be helpful and motivating, and shame the perspective that *I am wrong*, which can be debilitating and paralyzing.[73] When we have critical or perfectionistic parts of ourselves that spew inner negativity and then shameful parts that absorb these thoughts as gospel, finding love and happiness in ourselves can feel nearly impossible. I've come to see our inner critic as a form of emotional autoimmunity. When someone has an autoimmune condition, the immune system goes into overdrive and the body starts attacking itself instead of protecting itself from outside invasion. When we inquire into the motivation of the inner critic, it is usually a part of us that wants to protect us, keep us safe or have us be successful, but its methods are actually self-harming and counterproductive to its protective intention. Shame is like a weakened immune system that will catch an emotional cold through even the smallest of insults, neutral feedback or questioning from another. Even though the part of us experiencing shame often feels powerless, it is quite powerful in its capacity to eclipse our ability to connect with our self and with others. Shame can function like a form of deflated narcissism where any and all phenomena in the world are taken as evidence for how you are not worthy or how you are fundamentally failing, flawed or broken. Both the inner critic and shame can sabotage our relationships, because when we are living from these parts we are usually unable to relate authentically or take responsibility for our actions.

But remember that we are more than these parts. The inner critical and shameful parts of us can have a prominent impact through the ways they shape and distort our view of self, other and the world, and when in the driver's seat these parts can create much havoc, but they are not the totality of who we are. Just as our attachment styles are not the fullness of who we are, these parts are also just an aspect of ourselves that can be healed and transformed. Therapeutic modalities such as compassion-focused therapy, narrative therapy and Internal Family Systems use techniques to externalize and engage in dialogue with these parts to gain a better understanding of the ways in which they are either trying to protect us or are still holding pain, traumas and emotional burdens that can be released. When doing this kind of inner work, the grip that these parts have on us begins to loosen and more expressed delight can begin to shine through. As problematic parts get revised, unburdened, updated or transformed, other parts of our self that have been disowned or exiled, such as our self-esteem, voice, joy, enthusiasm, creativity or sexuality can also be reclaimed and integrated, thus fortifying our ability to better enact the strategies and positive self-talk that encourages self-interest, excitement, play and self-delight. It is just as important to cultivate the parts of us that can have self-compassion and help us function in securely attached ways as working with our critical and shameful parts, and I will touch on this in the next section.

Questions to Consider
- What does expressed delight look like for you right now?
- How could you increase your self-expressed delight?
- Do you struggle with critical and shameful inner parts that sabotage your ability to value and appreciate yourself?

- What would become more possible for you in regard to yourself and your relationships if expressed delight was more central to your inner experience?

Things to Try and to Experiment With
- Take yourself on a date or pamper yourself with something that you genuinely enjoy.
- Listen to self-hypnosis tracks or positive affirmations that are aligned with what you want to feel about yourself.
- Write yourself a love letter or make a list of all the things you appreciate about yourself.
- Start a gratitude practice and make sure to include yourself as the object of gratitude.
- Start working with your inner critic and shame through modalities such as Internal Family Systems, narrative therapy or compassion-focused therapy, which focus on inner parts work.
- Check out Rick Hanson's *Hardwiring Happiness* or Joe Dispenza's *Becoming Supernatural*, which both focus on how to create positive changes within your inner landscape.
- Start to identify the parts of you that do function in secure ways and focus on how to make them more prominent in your life. What daily practices or perspectives can you take on that bring your preferred expression of self more to the front and center in your life?
- Let yourself laugh and seek out humor.

A: Attuning to Yourself

Attunement is at the heart of secure attachment. In its absence, attachment security ceases to be possible. When there are early childhood attachment ruptures, requisite developments in a person's ability to tune into themself and regulate their inner states can become hindered. When our childhood needs are not met from the outside and our attachment figures are unable to help us learn how to identify and label our inner experiences in order to make sense of them and soothe ourselves, as adults we can then struggle with knowing how to feel our own feelings, identify our own needs, and calm down our own body, mind and heart in the way a nurturing caretaker would have. We can also run into considerable relational difficulty when we continue to have an "outside-in" approach to getting our needs met, expecting that our partners act as a substitute for our own inner nurturer. When we are able to tune in and tend to our needs from the inside first, we may still seek outward support, comfort and guidance from our partners, but our fundamental well-being and sense of being OK are not dependent on it.

When applied to the self, attunement is our ability to turn inward in order to become receptive and aware of our interior world. Self-attunement is the inner inquiry into what you are feeling, needing, thinking and experiencing. Self-attunement facilitates self-knowing, which furthers our ability to self-regulate and soothe our own physiological and emotional states, as well as respond appropriately to our environment. Regardless of a person's specific attachment style, people with attachment insecurity will all struggle to some degree with emotional regulation and self-soothing. People with more attachment anxiety tend to seek outward regulation from others—they want to be taken care of, try to overprocess with partners, look for someone fix or take away what they're going through, or can even seek someone else to just tell them what to do. People with an anxious attachment style can struggle with being able to hold and sit with their own feelings and so, like a game of emotional hot potato, they try to pass off their emotions to their partners in order to diffuse their own discomfort. Seeking this external regulation from others is often at the exclusion of their own self-regulation and their own sense of self.

People functioning from a dismissive attachment style steer clear of trying to emotionally regulate with others because, in many ways, they don't even see it as a possibility. The co-regulation that a child needs and would experience with an attachment figure was not available to them, so they learned to take care of themselves by disengaging from others and taking space to regulate. From the outside, it may look like people with avoidant attachment are able to self-regulate well since they are comfortable on their own, but usually they are not actually self-attuning and self-soothing as much as they are autoregulating—that is, partaking in activities that are more about zoning out or tuning out in order to dissociate from their internal states than tuning into and intentionally working with their internal states.

Types of Regulation

Auto-Regulation (It just happens)	• Self-stimulation or self-soothing done more automatically than consciously. • Autoregulation is done alone, so there is no interpersonal stress. • Can be similar to overfocusing on an object or task and can be dissociative or zoning out. Examples: Thumb-sucking, averting eye contact, reading, doing art, watching TV, alcohol, drugs, masturbating, daydreaming, overeating, swiping or scrolling on your phone.
External Regulation (You do it)	• Reaching for another to help regulate and soothe you. • Interactive, but only focusing on one person attuning to the other at a time. • Can overfocus on either the self or on the other. Examples: Being held and soothed by a caregiver, talking with a friend about your problems, listening to a live talk or music, getting a massage.
Interactive Regulation (We do it)	• Mutual or co-regulation with another where both people are regulating each other. • Skin-to-skin and eye-to-eye contact. • Both people are attuning to each other. Examples: Dancing with a partner, sex, having a mutual dialogue, musicians playing together, cooking together.
Self-Regulation (I do it)	• Regulating one's own state through active or intentional techniques that are self-soothing or stimulating. • Ability to exhibit self-control through managing bodily or emotional impulses. Examples: Calming down through breath control, mental techniques (e.g., reframing), muscle relaxation, vocal control. Some of the autoregulation behaviors can also be examples of self-regulation when they are intentional.

TABLE 9.1: Types of regulation, adapted from Stan Tatkin's "The Four Regulation (Self-Care) Strategies" from *We Do: Saying Yes to a Relationship of Depth, True Connection, and Enduring Love.*

People with a preoccupied style learned that in order to survive they needed to be vigilant about reaching out towards others, often at the expense of losing their sense of self, whereas people with dismissive or fearful-avoidant attachment styles learned the danger or futility of reaching out to others and so in retreating into themselves they lose their sense of other. In my practice, I see that regardless of a person's starting point, all of those with insecure attachment styles need support with knowing themselves better. People with insecure attachment need guidance in connecting more with their authentic needs, preferences and desires instead of defaulting into their more reflexive insecure defense mechanisms. Just as we need techniques that support us in quieting down and transforming our inner critic, we also need strategies that enhance our inner nurturer. Even when we haven't experienced nurturing from others, we still have an innate caregiving behavioral system that we can access and animate through practice. With self-compassion we can learn how to re-parent ourselves in ways we may have never received. All of the insecure styles will benefit from practicing self-attunement and learning how to truly self-regulate and self-soothe, rather than turning to distraction, deflection or avoidance. There can be a healing effect of being with discomfort, of contacting pain or pleasure without collapsing or disconnecting, that can allow people to access their own inner safe haven and secure base. Each of the insecure attachment styles also has some specific ways that they can further grow.

Ways that each of the insecure attachment styles can focus on growth:

Preoccupied

- Focus on strengthening your sense of self. You can begin to do this through identifying your own values, needs, likes and dislikes. What makes you tick, what are your dreams, talents, callings and purposes? Exploring personality tests like the enneagram or Myers-Briggs as well as knowing your love languages can also support this process.

- Boundaries, boundaries, boundaries! The anxious style tends to have more porous boundaries regarding input where other people are defining you, as well as on the output where you are inserting yourself too far into another person's emotional, physical or mental space. Creating more distinct, but not rigid, boundaries is important for learning how to stay in your own skin while being connected to others, rather than leaving yourself behind to be with others. Also, be aware of not letting other people occupy more of your internal space than you are.

- Recognize when you are abandoning yourself and learn techniques to come back into your own body and your own internal world. Body-based meditations and awareness practices can support you being better able to inhabit your own body.

- When co-regulating with partners, make sure that it is reciprocal and that you are not either over-caretaking at the expense of yourself or asking them to take care of you without regard for themselves.

- Work on being able to receive love. Even though someone with a preoccupied attachment style is more likely to complain that they are not getting enough love or attention, when it is given, they

often struggle with how to really let it in and receive
it. What obstacles or defensive mechanisms arise
when love, connection or nourishment is actually
being offered?

- Learn techniques to ground and work with your
anxiety instead of projecting it onto others or
directing your anxiety into the relational space.

Dismissive

- Needing support does not mean that you are weak,
needy or less than. People with this style can carry
a lot of toxic shame about needing others or having
any needs at all. Can you begin to accept that
wanting support or attention from others is alright,
even healthy, and not a negative reflection on your
abilities, competence or independence? I invite you
to allow the fullness of your humanness.
- With people who are safe, begin to take the risk of
revealing and sharing more of yourself so that people
can get a glimpse into your internal world. This
could take the form of relaxing some of your more
rigid boundaries and letting more of yourself out.
- Also work on letting people *in* more. Let people
have an impact on how you feel or allow their
experiences, needs, opinions or feedback to impact
your perspective.
- Work with transforming your self-reliant parts
through relying more on or leaning into your partners for support, nourishment and connection. It's
OK to start with small requests. I almost had a panic
attack the first time I asked my partner to pick up a
yogurt for me on the way over to my house. To me,

this seemed like an unreasonable ask, even though he was the one who asked me if I needed anything from the store that he was already stopping at.

- Wake up your body. Often people with the dismissive style exist primarily in their heads, being cut off from the neck down. Exploring movement practices, body-based meditations and awareness practices can help you wake up your body and begin to allow and tolerate a whole range of sensations and feelings.

- Learn how to articulate your feelings and needs. This is easier said than done, since this is a developmental capacity that you have to learn and grow, not just an easy behavioral shift or a switch that you can turn on. Please be patient with yourself.

Fearful-Avoidant

People with this style either experience alternating aspects of the dismissive and preoccupied styles, or both can occur simultaneously, so try some or all of the above suggestions for both the preoccupied and the dismissive styles that feel relevant to you. In addition to the above suggestions you can also:

- Focus on building an internal sense of safety where you have a bodily felt sense that you are safe and that you can relax, even if it is just with yourself at first. When there has been trauma, this usually requires the support of a professional.

- Build an inner sense of protection. Doing inner work can support you in identifying the parts of you that can protect you that are not harmful to you or others. It can also be helpful to invite these protective parts to become more central to your daily experience. Remembering a person or a time when you felt protected and allowing that memory to come alive in your body can support you in having a tangible somatic experience of protection that you can access when you need it. Even when people have had parents who were harmful or not protective, there is usually someone we can identify as having felt a sense of protection with, whether it was another relative, a teacher or someone in our community. If you are truly unable to access any memories, people or times when you felt protected, explore the mythical, fictional or spiritual realms, where there might be a character that you resonate with or a spiritual and archetypal energy that you can associate protection with.

- Learn about the signs of being in an abusive relationship as well as the signs and signals that someone is gaslighting, manipulating or acting in narcissistic ways. People functioning in this style can unintentionally normalize what is abusive and unhealthy and so need help in being able to explicitly distinguish what is healthy and unhealthy, what is abusive or caring and what is addictive or genuine.

- Surround yourself with people who truly mean well, are more securely attached and who want to be a support for you in your healing process.

Questions to Consider
- What does self-attunement look like for you?
- In what ways do you autoregulate or try to use others to regulate, so that you don't have to self-regulate?
- What would self-regulation look like for you?

- How would you like to increase your self-attunement and self-regulation?
- What is your relationship with your inner nurturer like and how can this part of you become more front and center in your relationship with yourself?

Things to Try and to Experiment With
- Spend quiet time by yourself.
- Practice mindfulness or breath-based exercises that help you tune into your body, heart and mind.
- Try self-compassion meditations.
- Experiment with journaling.
- Try self-hypnosis techniques.
- Learn self-empathy practices that help you to identify your feelings and needs and give yourself what you need as best you can.
- Figure out what different kinds of sensory input, such as sights, smells, sounds, touches or tastes, are calming or irritating to you and have certain smells or types of music available for when you are needing some self-support.
- Develop a relationship with your inner nurturer and, if needed, work with a practitioner to support you in this process.

R: Rituals and Routines for a Secure Self

Any secure relationship with yourself will include the rituals and routines that support you in your self-care and sanity. If we refer back to early childhood, it is easy to see how children thrive when there is enough structure and predictable routine for the different needs of their bodies and the various transitions within a day. As adults, this does not change. There are natural rhythms to our cycles of sleeping, eating, resting and having sex that suffer when ignored. Both men and women have hormonal cycles that fluctuate, impacting our mood, mental acuity, how sensitive we feel and how short or long our fuse for anger and frustration will be. Secure attachment with self includes knowing your inner rhythms (biological, emotional and mental) and figuring out what routines and daily rituals best support you to be in alignment with your own needs and pacing.

Larger, more intentional or ceremonial rituals also play an important part in your relationship with yourself. Rituals and rites of passage that are intended to initiate us into higher aspects of self or mature us into adulthood are all but lost in our Western culture, and the few that remain (confirmation of faith, the bar/bat mitzvah, marriage, the sweet sixteen or *quinceañera*, high school or college graduation) have been co-opted and commercialized so as to divest them of their traditional purpose, which was a *literal* change of consciousness for which the people involved had been physically, mentally and emotionally prepared, leaving only a vestigial symbolic importance. The loss of the impact of such culturally approved rites of passage means that the millennia-old practice of having a ritual-based matrix in place to assist us with adjusting to life events (and the accompanying change of consciousness required to accommodate those events) is often no longer available to us.

The traditional *ashrama* system in Hinduism, for example, specifies that after having been a student and a householder and fulfilling one's earthly responsibilities in the culture, a person should undergo the ritual of *sannyasa* (renunciation of worldly affairs) and shift consciousness towards preparation for giving up their body at the time of death. Without such a custom, we are often left to deal with the anxiety and stress of end-of-life issues without a supportive community or a clearly understood cultural context that contributes to our psychic security.

The modern "psychedelic renaissance"—when Westerners travel to South and Central America and partake in ayahuasca rituals for the purposes of healing and self-discovery—also underscores the lack of such important rituals in our own cultural milieu, while simultaneously demonstrating how far people will go to restore the much-needed self-awareness such rituals potentially provide. When examining the apparent emptiness of much sacramental or ritual activity in the West and its lack of ability in modern times to alter the consciousness of the person undergoing it, many philosophers (Carl Jung and Terence McKenna, among others) have noted that over time, sacraments have become merely symbolic. Fortunately, nothing stops us from revitalizing older rituals or even creating new ones to assist us with living successfully and happily in the world we inhabit.

When focusing on establishing a more secure relationship with yourself, one of the most influential routines we can implement is what I refer to as self-alignment practices. When we start to clear away the debris of our insecure attachment styles, we reveal a secure self that can be cultivated and aligned with. Many of us already have a sense of the parts of us that we might refer to as our better self or higher self, or what I refer to as my secure self or aligned self (this is the part of me that is aligned with my better skills, values, visions and morals). When we actively engage in practices that bring these parts of us to the forefront, we are rewiring ourselves to resonate more easily with a self that is more peaceful, joyful, loving and accepting. If we give fuel to a negative self in the form of constant or obsessive mental reinforcement of that version of ourselves, then we strengthen that construct. But it also stands to reason that the opposite is true. If we live in alignment with our most secure, loving and happy self and practice living through the lens of the qualities about us that are remarkable, then we stabilize that construct until that is who we will eventually become.

Questions to Consider
- What routines and rituals do you have that support you in your well-being and self-care?
- What routines and rituals do you need to add into your day or week that would even better support you in your well-being and self-care?
- Are there larger rituals or rites of passage that you would like to experience?
- What practices do you already do that align you with your better or secure self?
- What practices could you take on to align yourself with the secure you?

Things to Try and to Experiment With
- If you could design your ideal day or week based on your natural rhythms of sleeping, eating, resting, connecting or having sex, what would that look like? Experiment with adjusting some of your day or week to better accommodate these preferences.
- Imagine your ideal day or week that includes self-care activities and rituals that support you in secure functioning with yourself. Start to add some of these

routines to your daily or weekly activities, even if you start with something as small as five minutes a day.

- Plan larger rituals or rites of passage that you think might assist you in your journey. A quick internet search may give you some ideas. There are also a variety of group ritualistic practices available in many places, ranging from silent retreats to group shamanic drumming. Find one you think would be helpful and experiment.

- Check out Dr. Daniel P. Brown's Ideal Parent Figure exercise, which can support you in rewiring your past and feeling more secure in the present.[74]

- Give definition to your secure self. What does this part of you look like? How does this part of you behave? What values and principles guide this part of you? Explore different techniques and practices to support you in aligning with your more secure self.

T: Turning Towards Yourself after Inner Conflict and Doing Trigger Management

In the previous chapter, the T in HEART was about turning towards each other after conflict, focusing on how we repair with our partners when there have been disconnections, fights or misunderstandings. Repairing with ourselves is also essential. How we treat ourselves when we have made a mistake, when there is an internal battle between different parts of ourselves or when we have fallen short of our own standards, ethics or expectations, is imperative in building a strong inner secure foundation. In the section on expressed delight with yourself, I have already spoken about the importance of working with one's inner critic, which is equally relevant here as well. When your inner critic is beating you up, bullying you or injecting self-doubt into your consciousness, knowing how to work with this part of you and reclaim your power from it is enormously helpful. Left unchecked, our inner critic can further feed cycles of attachment anxiety and avoidance that can be destructive and paralyzing.

One important aspect in working with your inner critic and being able to reduce the impact of its harsh ways is learning how to translate its message. When we engage in dialogue with this part of us and inquire into why it is so persistent, more times than not, we find that it is trying to protect us—from harm, from looking bad, from being disliked or from failing in some way. Stated more positively, this part of us is usually trying to keep us safe and to assure us that we are getting some form of love, acceptance or social inclusion. The irony here is that even though its intention is positive, its methods of self-scolding, shoulding or shaming are seriously counterproductive to the cause. However, when we are able to identify the positive and protective intention that our inner critic has for us, we can gain the power to translate its intention.

Let's look at an example. When I hear my inner critic say that bringing up that I'm hurt by something to my partner is petty of me and that I'm being overly sensitive or needy, I can get curious about what this part of me is trying to do. In this case, my inner critic is trying to keep me from getting further hurt based on the fear that if I reveal myself, I won't be cared for and listened to in the way I need and I will ultimately lose the relationship for having needs (yes, this is a history of neglect speaking). At that moment, if I am mindful of it, I can first give myself what I need, which is acknowledgment and acceptance of what I'm feeling and some self-care. I am able to translate the inner critic and then be my own safe haven through some self-connection and soothing. This then allows me to approach my partner from a position of advocating for my needs, rather than from the voice of the inner critic.

Dick Schwartz, the developer of the Internal Family Systems Model, makes an important distinction that in relationships we can speak *for* our parts, but should be careful not to speak *from* them.[75] When I speak directly *from* my inner critic, I am likely to be blaming my partner or myself, which pushes us further apart. If I am able to speak *for* the part of me that has been hurt, more possibility opens up for both of us to be understood and get our needs met. Initially, doing the work of translating our inner critic takes diligence. The inner critic is usually a persistent old habit that is well-established in the neural networks of our brains, so expecting change overnight is not realistic. But identifying the inner critic's larger intention, not believing what it says and translating its voice over and over again eventually pays off and is well worth the effort.

Managing triggers is another important component of creating secure attachment with yourself. Triggers are events that happen in the present that activate painful or traumatic experiences from our past that have some resemblance to what's happening in the present moment. When this happens, it's extremely difficult to tease apart what we are reacting to in this moment that is real and legitimate and what past stuff is coloring our interpretation and reactivity.

Millions of years of evolution have wired into us a stress response that is meant to keep us alive in life-threatening situations. When we feel threatened, our primitive reptilian brain and our emotional mammalian brain systems fire up to either fight and defend ourselves, flee and quickly escape, freeze and play dead, or appease and submit. This has been a very necessary system to help us first detect if our environment is safe or dangerous and then to instantaneously react accordingly. But, interestingly, our brains can't distinguish between a physical threat to our life and an emotional or mental threat to our ego, identity or worldview. So, when we think we've made a mistake, when someone challenges our worldview or when we presume that someone is going to judge or reject us, we can get triggered into a fight/flight/freeze/appease response. In today's world, it's not a ferocious animal that poses a threat, but your partner on the couch texting with someone else or your date being 20 minutes late. But your body can respond in the same way as if your life were threatened.

Our bodies were not designed for the daily stressors of modern life or to be triggered on a regular basis, so it's important to our mental and physical health that we learn to manage triggers. I've come to see trigger management as a basic life skill that we all need for the health and success of any relationship—whether with a family member, friend, co-worker, parent or romantic partner. Then I started to work with nonmonogamous people and I transitioned to being polyamorous myself, and understanding our triggers and knowing how to defuse our reactivity became even more relevant. In nonmonogamy, we need more skills around our triggers because as the number of people increases, the constellation of intimate relationships complexifies. For many, this relational complexity can be very beautiful and rich—it can feed those of us who want deeper community and tribe—but it can also bring many more opportunities for our triggers to get activated with each different lover, metamour, and family member or friend of your partners that comes along.

In nonmonogamy, we can also get completely blind-sided with triggers that we didn't even know we had—triggers that never would have shown up within the context of monogamy. That said, my experience has taught me that our triggers can be a gift. Of course, it never feels like a gift in the moment of being triggered, but if we can approach our triggers with curiosity and learn to shift into being responsive instead of acting from knee-jerk reactivity, our triggers become an amazing opportunity to strengthen and deepen our relationship with ourselves and with our partners. Just as how we want to speak *for* our parts instead of *from* them, we also want to learn how to respond *to* our triggers instead of reacting *from* them. Understanding and inquiring into your triggers can be a powerful way to heal past pain and transform outdated beliefs or stories that you might still be stuck in. Working with your triggers can free you up to live your life and conduct your relationships based on your preferred expressions of self—living from love, connection and choice instead of automatic reactions.

Questions to Consider
- How do you treat yourself when you make a mistake or fall short of your own standards and expectations?
- How do you respond to yourself when you have an inner conflict?

- How would you like to treat yourself differently?
- What would become possible for you if you did this?
- How frequently are you getting triggered and how does this impact you?
- What could you do to better manage your triggers, both preventively and during an actual trigger?

Things to Try and to Experiment With
- When your inner critic arises, try engaging in dialogue with it instead of just believing it. Ask what it wants for you and if it is trying to protect you in any way. You can do this verbally, internally or in writing. Keep engaging with it until you get to a positive intention that it is holding for you. Once you have this positive intention, you can then experiment with translating the inner critic any time it arises again.
- Seek support through books, programs, training or with a professional to work with your inner critic and to manage your triggers.
- No matter how triggered, anxious or out of control you feel, it's important to know that you can change your arousal system and calm yourself. Mindful deep belly breathing (even for just 60 seconds) is an effective way to decrease heightened arousal and return your body to a state of homeostasis.
- Experiment with cognitive reappraisal or cognitive reframing techniques to reinterpret a situation and change your emotional response to it. For example, if you haven't heard from a partner for an unusual amount of time, instead of thinking that they are uninterested in you or pulling away, you might instead wonder if they are busy doing something

important or whether their phone battery died. Or if you are struggling with a partner or metamour, you can try to see the situation from their point of view and consider how they may also be struggling in this situation.

- Check out Deirdre Fay's workbook *Becoming Safely Embodied: A Skills-Based Approach to Working with Trauma and Dissociation.*
- Check out Bonnie Weiss and Jay Earley's book, *Freedom from Your Inner Critic: A Self-Therapy Approach.*

In this chapter we have covered how to create earned secure attachment and how to apply the HEART of being polysecure to yourself. Changing deeply ingrained habits and beliefs is not easy or instantaneous, but it is possible. Doing this kind of work can be life-changing and well worth the effort. However, there is a paradox in this process of working with our attachment. Some people might advise you to first create a secure attachment with yourself before you can have secure relationships with others, or they might say that you need to experience secure attachment with others before you can have it with yourself. When we are talking about adults I believe that both can be true. What you've gone through both as a child and as an adult, how pain-free or painful your nonmonogamy journey has been and where you are in your personal growth process will dictate what's best for you. Some of us need to take a pause on dating and turn inward to heal, deconstruct and rebuild ourselves. This can allow us to bring forward a more fortified and healthy self that is able to relate in secure ways with others. Others may need to first have enough positive experiences where we feel seen, loved and met before embarking on inner work. These experiences can build a certain outer relational security that then can enable us to have enough self-worth, courage and capacity to look inward. These processes can alternate back and forth or can also occur simultaneously, where we are both in relationships that are healing and supportive to us and at the same time doing inner attachment work as well. Whichever of the polysecure HEARTS paths is for you, please allow it to unfold in the ways that work best and make the most sense for you and your relationships, knowing that it will probably be more circuitous than linear.

CHAPTER TEN
COMMON QUESTIONS AND FINAL THOUGHTS

BEFORE WE END THIS BOOK, I want to cover a few questions that I am asked frequently enough to make them worth addressing. Then I will offer my final words to you.

How many nonmonogamous attachment-based relationships can I have?

I get this question a lot, and, probably to your disappointment, I don't have a single quantifiable number to give you. Maybe in the future, there will be research that indicates the ideal number of attachment figures you can have while nonmonogamous, but I'd still be cautious of this because what I've seen is that it really depends on circumstances. There are many factors that will impact how many partners you can fully enter into a secure attachment–based relationship with. How demanding of your time and attention is your work? Do you have kids? If so, how many and how old are they? Do you care for elderly parents or other adults? Are you in school? How stable is your living situation? How's your health? Do you or your partners have any special needs? Where are you in your healing process regarding trauma and attachment insecurity? Are there certain hobbies or passions that are very important for you to pursue or make time for? Are you in a major life transition (e.g., divorce, moving house, a career change, gender transition or leaving an organized religion)? Are you in a certain phase of life that makes it easier or harder to have partners? These are just some of the factors that can impact how much emotional bandwidth a person has for secure relationships. It's not just about how polysaturated you are, but how life-saturated you are.

In the nonmonogamous world there is a popular saying that *love is infinite, but time and resources are not*. This saying highlights the paradox of ultimate versus relative reality—love is not a finite resource, so it is possible for us to love more than one person at a time, but we are all in bodies that are limited to the relative realities of space and time, so having infinite partners is not actually possible. When thinking about attachment-based relationships, this phrase is extremely relevant and can be adapted to say that *love is infinite, but secure attachment is not*. Since not all of your relationships have to be attachment-based, you may have several, even many, romantic or sexual partners. But it is important to be honest and realistic about how many people you have the time and resources to invest in the HEART of being polysecure with before you begin to compromise or dilute your other attachment-based relationships. Additionally, if you prioritize secure attachment with yourself, does this change, whether through enhancing or reducing, what you can offer others?

Should we close our relationship when there are attachment problems?

Again, it depends. I've seen both ends of the spectrum—closing an open relationship can cause damage both inside and outside of the relationship, but staying open when there are clear attachment problems can also cause irreparable damage to the people or relationships struggling with attachment insecurity. Some people are quick to advise a struggling couple to close up, to just focus on each other and to take the time to heal their attachment issues. If that feels like the right decision for you and your partner, then great! There are times when I have seen this as the best option for an individual or couple, but be cautious of applying monogamous advice to a polyamorous context. Attachment issues do not just show up in the early stages of a monogamous couple opening up, but also with people who are solo poly and with people who have been practicing forms of nonmonogamy for years, so please beware of jumping to closing a relationship as the attachment cure-all.

Through working with individuals, couples and polycules, I have seen people try many different courses of action when there is attachment insecurity in a polyamorous context. These options range from completely closing up a relationship, to taking a temporary dating pause or having certain relationship limits, to staying completely open. Each of these has its pros and cons, with certain restrictions and certain freedoms. While it is extremely difficult to experience polyinsecurity, is also difficult to be asked to change your behavior to support your insecure partner. When deciding which of these potential options would be best for you and your relationships, it is good to remember that attachment work is more about the marathon than the sprint. Two important factors to consider are:

1. How severe is the attachment insecurity? Is it mild, moderate or severe to the point of interfering with functionality, well-being or mental health?

2. How much damage could be caused for the partners who are not experiencing attachment insecurity, based on how open or closed an individual or pairing of partners decides they are going to be? There is an important distinction here between *damage* and *discomfort*. Some of the below options might not be comfortable for everyone involved, but they should not be damaging. Even if some of these options are uncomfortable and not what you would necessarily choose in your ideal situation, they should still be considered as temporary choices or compromises that you are willing to make because they feel worth it for the health of your relationship or polycule, versus options that are damaging to you, your partners or your metamours.

Closing Up:

When attachment insecurity is at play, one option is to temporarily close up. Closing up typically looks like both you and your partner getting off the dating apps and taking a complete break from seeing any people you have been talking to or even dating. Basically, you're going back to monogamy for a moment. Temporarily closing up to focus on healing your attachment can be helpful, especially when there is more severe attachment insecurity. The caveats here are that attachment healing does not happen overnight and there will probably never be a point where you are 100 percent healed and feel absolutely ready to open up again, so at some point you will have to face the discomfort of moving forward into nonmonogamy. Ideally you will only do this when you and/or your partner have enough inner foundation and interpersonal strength to weather the storm. I've seen closing up work best in the following situations:

- You are currently single and you decide to refrain from dating or entering into a relationship until you feel more capable and ready to relate from a secure place.

- You are in a relationship that is new to opening up where one or both partners are experiencing attachment insecurity and neither of you has any other relationships that you would be deserting or harming by closing up.

- You are *not* new to nonmonogamy and you and your one partner are in a phase where you don't have other relationships.

- You are *not* new to nonmonogamy and you have multiple partners and metamours, but they are genuinely alright with taking a break while you do the attachment work needed in your primary relationship. Typically, these other relationships are not as attachment-based.

Taking a Pause:

A few steps further along from completely closing up is taking a pause. Unlike when an individual or a couple completely closes up and stops pursuing any other relationships, a person or a couple taking a pause may maintain some of their current connections, but press the pause button on progressing in those relationships for a certain amount of time. In this scenario, a person might still talk and message with partners as friends or spend time together in person, but they are temporarily stepping back from the more romantic or sexual dimensions of those relationships. For some people this can be a very supportive option since you don't have to completely let go of certain connections that may be of importance to you, but you can also temporarily have a rest from the added attachment stress of multiple partners. One person I worked with called her version of a pause her attachment sabbatical. She informed all of her partners that she had no intention of ending or changing their relationships, but she was choosing to be out of contact for six weeks to do her own inner attachment work. After six weeks, she planned to return to the relationships as if she had just been away on a retreat during that time. In her case, all of her partners were able to accommodate her sabbatical and they agreed to only make contact in case of an emergency. I've seen a pause work when:

- The person initiating the pause is doing so with partners who they are less entwined with or committed to.
- The person initiating the pause *does* have partners who they are more entwined with or committed to, but these partners are able to fully consent to the pause, usually because they have other partners to turn to for romance or sex, they are in a very secure place themselves and/or the pause is temporary enough that they are willing to wait.
- People are more oriented to relationship anarchy or relationship fluidity and everyone involved is able to smoothly shift back and forth from being more or less romantically/sexually involved.

Creating a Vessel:

When there is attachment insecurity within a polycule, I've seen people adopt a form of temporary polyfidelity where all current relationships stay as they are, but no new partners are added to the mix. This may mean either that all partners are polyfidelitous for a certain amount of time or that just some are. A married polyamorous couple that I work with coined their version of this "the vessel." In their case, the husband was experiencing a more severe form of attachment insecurity that was rooted in his childhood, but was getting repeatedly triggered by his wife having two other partners and several potential suitors in the wings. When he and I first started our sessions together he wasn't sure if he could do *any* version of polyamory, but as we identified the root of his struggles, the idea of a temporary vessel became a more preferable option than scrapping polyamory all together. In their own words:

The husband:

> *Coming to polyamory from swinging, I was accustomed to the safety of sharing experiences with my wife. The first year of polyamory left me floundering. Instead of bonding with my wife, I felt abandoned by the ease with which she could navigate polyamory and the difficulty I had in finding the sensual and sexual experiences that I also craved.*
> *My anxious attachment style was fostered during my traumatic childhood, but definitely tickled by the multi-weekly dates that my wife was going on, as I stayed home with the children and tried to put a good and supportive face on. One*

image that kept occurring to me was two birds in flight, with the difference in their altitude representing the difference in their polyamorous experiences. My wife constantly soared higher than me, and at times I felt as though she'd lose sight of me, abandoning me for others and other experiences.

The concept of a vessel came about during one of my therapy sessions with Jess. I realized that it was the expansion of the number of partners that my wife had that was more anxiety-producing than the depth and closeness that she had with her current partners, which for me was beautiful and non-threatening. It was the anticipation of the breadth of partners that was triggering me, not depth.

The vessel that my wife and I negotiated was four months long, where she continued to be with her two other partners in addition to me, but she would not add any new partners to our polycule. The idea was she could experience as much depth in those months with the two partners as she wanted, but she wouldn't look to expand her breadth with new partners during this time.

When she fully consented I immediately relaxed. With her on board, I stopped trying to manage her polyamory, and I was able to in earnest do the hard emotional healing and attachment work that I needed to do to better ground and align myself. I entered into a short, but beautiful, relationship of my own, and spent much less time worried about the distance between us in flight, and focused on keeping my flight steady and with less turbulence. That said, the negative aspect of the vessel was the truth that I had put rules around how my wife could practice poly, and

I had to sit with this. On balance I'd say the pros definitely outweighed the cons. Before the vessel I wasn't even sure if we could stay married.

There was definitely some angst on my end when the vessel's period came to an end, but having an end time was important for a few reasons: it gave me the opportunity to test my newfound alignment, which lifted my self-esteem; it allowed for us to practice polyamory in a less hierarchical way that is important for my wife's ability to have her own agency; and it gives us a moment in time that we can reflect back to with gratitude. It was a very helpful tool, not a permanent design.

The wife:

Coming up with the vessel was an important turning point for us. It gave us a temporary container to get into a secure place, which was highly needed. For me the pros of the vessel were:

» *The vessel allowed my husband space to catch his breath, which had a big impact on me.*

» *It gave me a concrete way of showing my husband I care about his needs and feelings. It was a way for me to show him that he is a priority to me.*

» *I was no longer crossing unspoken boundaries and therefore triggering my husband. So, for the first time, I had clear boundaries to follow!*

» *It increased the security of my husband and my attachment to him.*

» *The vessel made a dramatic decrease in my husband being triggered, which was the most amazing thing.*

> » *We were losing each other, and with the vessel*
> *we were able to be "us" again.*

For me the cons of the vessel were:
> » *When my other relationships were not going*
> *as great and my husband's other relationships*
> *were going fabulously, I struggled with resent-*
> *ment in having the vessel.*
> » *It was challenging for me interacting with*
> *people who were outside the vessel, but whom I*
> *already had varying degrees of an established*
> *romantic or sexual relationship with.*

Given the pros and the cons, in the end, it was the
right choice for me, him and us.

Staying Open with No Restrictions:

When polyinsecurity is at play, another option is to *not*
change anything, staying completely open to current and
potential new partners while simultaneously working
through attachment insecurity. To be honest, I have not
yet seen this work in more severe cases of attachment
insecurity, but I have seen it work when people are experiencing mild to moderate attachment insecurity. I've also
seen this work when:

- Individuals and partners are getting professional
  support for their attachment struggles.
- Partners are highly motivated to work on their own
  attachment insecurity and are willing to do the
  HEARTS of being polysecure together.
- Partners are able to prioritize time together to do the
  needed healing work.

Final Words

Thank you for coming on this journey with me! While this book has now come to an end, I hope that your journey has not. For all the things that I have included in the book, there are just as many things that I have not, and I know with certainty that as the book finally goes off to print I will undoubtedly wake up in the middle of the night tormented by additional edits I should have made or entire sections that I should have added.

We have covered several different aspects of attachment, trauma, nonmonogamy and what you can do to become more polysecure. It is my hope that this book will have an influence on our understanding of attachment and trauma by articulating the different levels at which they are experienced. The nested model can be applied to many other areas of identity and marginalization.

I hope that this book will challenge the monogamous presupposition that attachment theory primarily functions under and that some of the concepts covered are beneficial to people both monogamous and nonmonogamous. Cultivating secure attachment with ourselves is a universally applicable concept, not just for people wanting to be polysecure, but for anyone wanting to have more fulfillment, security and empowerment with themselves and in their relationships, whatever their form.

There are still many questions regarding the attachment experiences of polyamorous partners that need to be researched and answered. In particular, I hope that this book will encourage others to pursue further research into how early childhood attachment does or does not correlate with being nonmonogamous as an adult, how long-term polyamorous partners experience attachment throughout the lifespans of their multiple relationships and how the initial attachment challenges that we face when transitioning to nonmonogamy possibly create post-attachment growth, similar to how trauma can initiate positive post-traumatic growth.

I know this book is not a panacea for everything related to attachment, trauma or nonmonogamy, but my hope is that it has given you enough insight, perspective and guidance on how to move forward from here. I also hope that you were able to see yourself reflected on some of these pages and that you have more clarity and compassion for yourself, your partners and your metamours. Although the wounds of your past may run deep and you may have had experiences that left you feeling broken, worthless, invisible, unloved or unaccounted for, healing is not out of your reach. I will not lie: the work to heal our personal traumas and attachment wounds and the effort needed to build polysecure relationships are not easy. It takes courage, devotion and perseverance, but please trust me in knowing that it is worth it. As we heal our past, we open up new possibilities for our future, and so it is also my hope that you are able to forge a new path forward, seeking any further support you need and relating to yourself and your loved ones in ever more polysecure ways.

With love and gratitude,
Jessica Fern

NOTES

1   M. Pieper and R. Bauer, "Polyamory and Mono-normativity: Results of an Empirical Study of Non-monogamous Patterns of Intimacy." Unpublished manuscript, 2005.

2   J. Bowlby, *Attachment and Loss: Vol 1. Attachment.* (New York: Basic Books, 1969).

3   M. D. Ainsworth, "The Development of Infant-Mother Attachment," *Review of Child Development Research,* 3 (1973): 1–94.

4   M. Mikulincer and P. R. Shaver, *Attachment in Adulthood (Second Edition): Structure, Dynamics and Change* (New York: Guilford Press, 2016).

5   Mikulincer and Shaver, *Attachment in Adulthood (Second Edition).*

6   S. Johnson, *Hold Me Tight: Seven Conversations for a Lifetime of Love* (New York: Little, Brown, 2008).

7   A. N. Schore, "The Right Brain Is Dominant in Psychotherapy." *Psychotherapy* 51, no. 3 (2014): 388–397.

8   Bowlby, *Attachment and Loss: Vol 1.*

9   Bowlby, *Attachment and Loss: Vol 1.*

10   D. Zeifman and C. Hazan, "Pair Bonds as Attachments: Reevaluating the Evidence," in *Handbook of Attachment: Theory, Research, and Clinical Applications*, eds. J. Cassidy and P.R. Shaver (New York: Guilford Press, 2018), 436–455; E. G. Hepper and K. B. Carnelley, "Attachment and Romantic Relationships: The Role of Models of Self and Other," in *The Psychology of Love (Vol. 1)*, ed. M. Paludi (Santa Barbara, CA: Praeger, 2012), 133–154; D. F. Selterman, A. N. Gesselman, and A. C. Moors, "Sexuality Through the Lens of Secure Base Attachment Dynamics: Individual Differences in Sexploration," PsyArXiv (2019), https://doi.org/10.31234/osf.io/zsg3x.

11   Zeifman and Hazan, "Pair Bonds as Attachments."

12   See J. A. Feeney, 2008; Mikulincer, Florian, Cowan, and Cowan, 2002; Mikulincer and Shaver, 2007, for reviews.

13   Frei and Shaver, 2002; Joireman, Needham, and Cummings, 2002; Mikulincer, Shaver, and Slav, 2006.

14   K. P. Mark, L. M. Vowels, and S. H. Murray, "The Impact of Attachment Style on Sexual Satisfaction and Sexual Desire in a Sexually Diverse Sample," *Journal of Sex and Marital Therapy* 44, no. 5 (2018): 450–458.

15   Selterman, Gesselman, and Moors, "Sexuality Through the Lens of Secure Base Attachment Dynamics."

16   Mikulincer and Shaver, *Attachment in Adulthood (Second Edition)*.

17   M. D. Ainsworth, M. C. Blehar, E. Waters, and S. Wall, *Patterns of Attachment: A Psychological Study of the Strange Situation* (Hillsdale, NJ: Erlbaum, 1978).

18   This list has been adapted from D. P. Heller and K. H. Payne, "Secure Attachment Parenting in the Digital Age," 2019, https://attachmentmastery.com/parenting.

19   N. L. Collins and S. J. Read, "Adult Attachment, Working
     Models, and Relationship Quality in Dating Couples,"
     Journal of Personality and Social Psychology 58,
     no. 4 (1990): 644–663; K. N. Levy, "Introduction:
     Attachment Theory and Psychotherapy: Attachment and
     Psychotherapy," *Journal of Clinical Psychology* 69, no. 11
     (2013): 1133–1135.

20   G. Birnbaum, "Attachment Orientations, Sexual
     Functioning, and Relationship Satisfaction in a
     Community Sample of Women," *Journal of Social and
     Personal Relationships* 24, no. 1 (2007): 21–35; B. Butzer
     and L. Campbell, "Adult Attachment, Sexual Satisfaction,
     and Relationship Satisfaction: A Study of Married
     Couples," *Personal Relationships* 15, no. 1 (2008):
     141–154.

21   D. Siegel, *Mindsight: The New Science of Personal
     Transformation* (New York: Bantam Books, 2010).

22   D. J. Wallin, *Attachment in Psychotherapy* (New York:
     Guilford Press, 2007).

23   Heller and Payne, "Secure Attachment Parenting in the
     Digital Age"; D. P. Brown and D. S. Elliot, *Attachment
     Disturbances in Adults: Treatment for Comprehensive
     Repair* (New York: W. W. Norton & Company, 2016).

24   L. Campbell, J. A. Simpson, J. Boldry, and D. A. Kashy,
     "Perceptions of Conflict and Support in Romantic
     Relationships: The Role of Attachment Anxiety," *Journal
     of Personality and Social Psychology* 88, no. 3 (2005):
     510–531; C. Hazan and P. Shaver, "Romantic Love
     Conceptualized as an Attachment Process," *Journal of
     Personality and Social Psychology* 52, no. 3 (1987):
     511–524.

25 G. E. Birnbaum, H. Reis, M. Mikulincer, O. Gillath, and A. Orpaz, "When Sex Is More than Just Sex: Attachment Orientations, Sexual Experience, and Relationship Quality," *Journal of Personality and Social Psychology* 91, no. 5 (2006): 929–943; A. Bogaert and S. Sadava, "Adult Attachment and Sexual Behavior," *Personal Relationships* 9, no. 2 (2002): 191–204.

26 M. Main and J. Solomon, "Discovery of a New, Insecure-Disorganized/Disoriented Attachment Pattern," in *Affective Development in Infancy*, eds. M. Yogman and T. B. Brazelton (Norwood, NJ: Ablex, 1986), 95–124.

27 Heller and Payne, "Secure Attachment Parenting in the Digital Age."

28 E. Aron, *The Highly Sensitive Person: How to Thrive When the World Overwhelms You* (New York: Carol Publishing, 1996).

29 Such as Mikulincer and Shaver, *Attachment in Adulthood (Second Edition)*; J. Cassidy and P. Shaver, *Handbook of Attachment: Theory, Research, and Clinical Applications, Third Edition* (New York: Guilford Press, 2016).

30 Main and Solomon, "Discovery of a New, Insecure-Disorganized/Disoriented Attachment Pattern."

31 A. Bartels and S. Zeki, "The Neural Basis of Romantic Love," *NeuroReport: For Rapid Communication of Neuroscience Research* 11, no. 17 (2000): 3829–3834; X. Xu, A. Aron, L. Brown, G. Cao, T. Feng, and X. Weng, "Reward and Motivation Systems: A Brain Mapping Study of Early-Stage Intense Romantic Love in Chinese Participants," *Human Brain Mapping* 32 (2011): 249–257.

32 B. A. Primack, A. Shensa, J. E. Sidani, E. O. Whaite,
    L. Y. Lin, D. Rosen, J. B. Colditz, A. Radovic, and E.
    Miller, "Social Media Use and Perceived Social Isolation
    Among Young Adults in the U.S.," *American Journal of
    Preventive Medicine* 53, no. 1 (2017): 1–8.

33 J. Galtung, "Violence, Peace, and Peace Research," *Journal
    of Peace Research* 6, no. 3 (1969): 167–191.

34 C. Cyr, E. M. Euser, M. J. Bakermans-Kranenburg,
    and M. H. Van Ijzendoorn, "Attachment Security
    and Disorganization in Mistreating and High-Risk
    Families: A Series of Meta-analyses," *Development and
    Psychopathology* 22, no. 1 (2010): 87–108.

35 N. Hazen, S. Allen, C. Christopher, T. Umemura, and D.
    Jacobvitz, "Very Extensive Nonmaternal Care Predicts
    Mother–Infant Attachment Disorganization: Convergent
    Evidence from Two Samples," *Development and
    Psychopathology* 27, no. 3 (2014): 1–13.

36 T. Fey, *Bossypants* (New York: Little, Brown, 2011).

37 B. Wray, "How Climate Change Affects Your Mental
    Health," TED Talk (2019), video, 7:54, https://www.ted
    .com/talks/britt_wray_how_climate_change_affects
    _your_mental_health?language=en.

38 Z. Woodbury, "Climate Trauma: Towards a New
    Taxonomy of Traumatology," *Ecopsychology* 11, no. 1
    (2019): 1–8.

39 T. Hübl, "The Pocket Project," https://thomashuebl.com
    /about/pocket-project/.

40 E. Perel, *Mating in Captivity* (New York, NY:
    HarperCollins, 2006).

41 M. Tafoya and B. Spitzberg, "The Dark Side of Infidelity: Its Nature, Prevalence, and Communicative Functions," in *The Dark Side of Interpersonal Communication*, eds. B. Spitzberg and W. Cupach (Routledge, 2009): 211–252; A. L. Vangelisti and M. Gerstenberger, "Communication and Marital Infidelity," in *The State of Affairs: Explorations in Infidelity and Commitment*, eds. J. Duncombe, K. Harrison, G. Allen, and D. Marsden (Mahwah, NJ: Lawrence Erlbaum, 2004).

42 A. C. Moors, J. L. Matsick, and H. A. Schechinger, "Unique and Shared Relationship Benefits of Consensually Nonmonogamous and Monogamous Relationships," *European Psychologist* 22, no. 1 (2017): 55–71.

43 M. Life, *Spiritual Polyamory* (Lincoln, NE: iUniverse, Inc., 2004), 87–95.

44 M. L. Haupert, A. N. Gesselman, A. C. Moors, H. E. Fisher, and J. R. Garcia, "Prevalence of Experiences with Consensual Nonmonogamous Relationships: Findings from Two National Samples of Single Americans," *Journal of Sex & Marital Therapy* 43, no. 5 (2017): 424–440.

45 E. C. Levine, D. Herbenick, and O. Martinez, "Open Relationships, Nonconsensual Nonmonogamy, and Monogamy Among U.S. Adults: Findings from the 2012 National Survey of Sexual Health and Behavior," *Archives of Sexual Behavior* 47, no. 5 (2018): 1439–1450; J. D. Rubin, A. C. Moors, J. L. Matsick, A. Ziegler, and T. D. Conley, "On the Margins: Considering Diversity Among Consensually Nonmonogamous Relationships." *Journal für Psychologie* 22, no. 1 (2014): 19–37.

46 T. D. Conley, J. L. Matsick, A. C. Moors, and A. Ziegler, "Investigation of Consensually Nonmonogamous Relationships: Theories, Methods, and New Directions," *Perspectives on Psychological Science* 12, no. 2 (2017): 205–232; University of Guelph, "Open Relationships Just as Satisfying as Monogamous Ones," ScienceDaily, June 28, 2018, www.sciencedaily.com /releases/2018/06/180628151713.htm

47 J. K. Mogilski, S. D. Reeve, S. C. A. Nicolas, S. H. Donaldson, V. E. Mitchell, and L. L. M. Welling, "Jealousy, Consent, and Compersion within Monogamous and Consensually Non-monogamous Romantic Relationships," *Archives of Sexual Behavior* 48, no. 2 (2019): 1811–1828, doi:10.1007/s10508–018–1286–4; Conley, Matsick, Moors, and Ziegler, "Investigation of Consensually Nonmonogamous Relationships."

48 S. Sinek, *Find Your Why: A Practical Guide for Discovering Purpose for You and Your Team* (New York: Portfolio/Penguin, 2011).

49 Moors, Matsick, and Schechinger, "Unique and Shared Relationship Benefits of Consensually Nonmonogamous and Monogamous Relationships."

50 A. C. Moors, J. Matsick, A. Ziegler, J. Rubin, and T. Conley, "Stigma Toward Individuals Engaged in Consensual Nonmonogamy: Robust and Worthy of Additional Research," *Analyses of Social Issues and Public Policy* 13, no. 1 (2013): 52–69, https://doi.org/10.1111 /asap.12020.

51 F. Veaux and E. Rickert, *More Than Two: A Practical Guide to Ethical Polyamory* (Portland, OR: Thorntree Press, 2014).

52 A. Nordgren, "The Short Instructional Manifesto for Relationship Anarchy," log.andie.se. Originally published as Relationsanarki i 8 punkter, Interacting Arts, 2006.

53 A. C. Moors, T. D. Conley, R. S. Edelstein, and W. J. Chopik, "Attached to Monogamy? Avoidance Predicts Willingness to Engage (But not Actual Engagement) in Consensual Nonmonogamy," *Journal of Social and Personal Relationships* 32, no. 2 (2014): 222–240.

54 G. Birnbaum, "Attachment and Sexual Mating: The Joint Operation of Separate Motivational Systems," in *Handbook of Attachment: Theory, Research, and Clinical Applications, Second Edition*, eds. J. Cassidy and P. A. Shaver (New York: Guilford Press, 2016).

55 Moors, Conley, Edelstein, and Chopik, "Attached to Monogamy?"

56 M. E. Bricker and S. G. Horne, "Gay Men in Long-Term Relationships: The Impact of Monogamy and Nonmonogamy on Relational Health," *Journal of Couple & Relationship Therapy* 6, no. 4 (2007): 27–47.

57 S. King, "Attachment Security: Polyamory and Monogamy A Comparison Analysis" (2014). Retrieved from UMI Dissertation Publishing, UMI 3581155.

58 A. C. Moors, W. S. Ryan, and W. J. Chopik, "Multiple Loves: The Effects of Attachment with Multiple Concurrent Romantic Partners on Relational Functioning," *Personality and Individual Differences* 147 (2019): 102–110

59 C. Power, "How Secure Functioning Can Help Polyamorous Couples," 2014, https://stantatkinblog .wordpress.com/2018/01/15/how-secure-functioning-can -help-polyamorous-couples.

60 J. A. Simpson and J. Belsky, "Attachment Theory within a Modern Evolutionary Framework," in *Handbook of Attachment: Theory, Research, and Clinical Applications, Third Edition*, eds. J. Cassidy and P. R. Shaver (New York: Guilford Press, 2018).

61 Johnson, *Hold Me Tight*.

62 Johnson, *Hold Me Tight*.

63 E. Sheff, *The Polyamorists Next Door: Inside Multiple Partner Relationships and Families* (Lanham, MD: Rowman and Littlefield, 2014); E. Sheff, "Polyphobia: Anti-Polyamorous Prejudice and Discrimination," 2017, https://www.psychologytoday.com/us/blog/the-polyamorists-next-door/201707/polyphobia

64 Sheff, "Polyphobia."

65 B. Van der Kolk, "Cumulative Effects of Trauma," Collective Trauma Online Summit, 2019, https://thomashuebl.com/event/collective-trauma-online-summit.

66 S. Joseph, "Growth Following Adversity: Positive Psychological Perspectives on Posttraumatic Stress," *Psihologijske Teme* 18, no. 2 (2009): 335–344.

67 R. G. Tedeschi and L. G. Calhoun, "Posttraumatic Growth: Conceptual Foundations and Empirical Evidence," *Psychological Inquiry* 15, no. 1 (2004): 1–18.

68 Bowlby, *Attachment and Loss: Vol 1*.

69 S. Johnson, "Intensive Course in Emotionally Focused Therapy with Sue Johnson: Attachment-Based Interventions for Couples in Crisis," Lesson Two, https://catalog.pesi.com/sales/bh_001234_eftintensive_011518_organic-78213

70 Brown and Elliot, *Attachment Disturbances in Adults*.

71   J. Gottman, J. S. Gottman, D. C. Abrams, and R. C. Abrams,
     Eight Dates: Essential Conversations for a Lifetime of Love
     (New York: Workman Publishing Company, 2018).

72   Siegel, *Mindsight.*

73   B. Brown, *Men, Women, and Worthiness: The Experience
     of Shame and the Power of Being Enough* (Audiobook;
     Boulder, CO: Sounds True, 2012).

74   Brown and Elliot, *Attachment Disturbances in Adults.*

75   R. C. Schwartz, *Internal Family Systems Therapy (The
     Guilford Family Therapy Series)* (New York: Guilford
     Press, 1995).

BIBLIOGRAPHY

Ainsworth, M. D. "The Development of Infant-Mother Attachment." *Review of Child Development Research*, 3 (1973): 1–94.

Ainsworth, M. D., M. C. Blehar, E. Waters, and S. Wall. *Patterns of Attachment: A Psychological Study of the Strange Situation*. Hillsdale, NJ: Erlbaum, 1978.

Allan, R., and A. Westhaver. "Attachment Theory and Gay Male Relationships: A Scoping Review." *Journal of GLBT Family Studies* 14, no. 4 (2018): 295–316.

Aron, E. *The Highly Sensitive Person: How to Thrive When the World Overwhelms You*. New York: Carol Publishing, 1996.

Bartels, A., and S. Zeki. "The Neural Basis of Romantic Love." *NeuroReport: For Rapid Communication of Neuroscience Research* 11, no. 17 (2000): 3829–3834.

Birnbaum, G. "Attachment and Sexual Mating: The Joint Operation of Separate Motivational Systems." In *Handbook of Attachment: Theory, Research, and Clinical Applications*, 2nd Edition, edited by J. Cassidy and P. A. Shaver, 464–483. New York: Guilford Press, 2016.

Birnbaum, G. "Attachment Orientations, Sexual Functioning, and Relationship Satisfaction in a Community Sample of Women." *Journal of Social and Personal Relationships* 24, no. 1 (2007): 21–35.

Birnbaum, G. E., H. Reis, M. Mikulincer, O. Gillath, and A. Orpaz. "When Sex Is More Than Just Sex: Attachment Orientations, Sexual Experience, and Relationship Quality." *Journal of personality and social psychology* 91, no. 5 (2006): 929–943.

Bogaert, A., and S. Sadava. "Adult Attachment and Sexual Behavior." *Personal Relationships* 9, no. 2 (2002): 191–204.

Bowlby, J. *Attachment and Loss: Vol 1. Attachment.* New York: Basic Books, 1969.

Bowlby, J. *Attachment and Loss, Vol. 2. Separation: Anxiety and Anger.* New York: Basic Books, 1973.

Bricker, M. E., and S. G. Horne. "Gay Men in Long-Term Relationships: The Impact of Monogamy and Nonmonogamy on Relational Health." *Journal of Couple & Relationship Therapy* 6, no. 4 (2007): 27–47

Brown, B. *Men, Women, and Worthiness: The Experience of Shame and the Power of Being Enough.* Audiobook. Boulder, CO: Sounds True, 2012.

Brown, D. P., and D. S. Elliot. *Attachment Disturbances in Adults: Treatment for Comprehensive Repair.* New York: W. W. Norton & Company, 2016.

Butzer, B., and L. Campbell. "Adult Attachment, Sexual Satisfaction, and Relationship Satisfaction: A Study of Married Couples." *Personal Relationships* 15, no. 1 (2008): 141–154.

Campbell, L., J. A. Simpson, J. Boldry, and D. A. Kashy. "Perceptions of Conflict and Support in Romantic Relationships: The Role of Attachment Anxiety." *Journal of Personality and Social Psychology* 88, no. 3 (2005): 510–531.

Cassidy, J., and P. Shaver. *Handbook of Attachment: Theory, Research, and Clinical Applications, Third Edition.* New York: Guilford Press, 2016.

Chapman, G. D. *The Five Languages of Apology: How to Experience Healing in All Your Relationships.* Chicago: Northfield Publishing, 2006.

Chapman, G. D. *The Five Love Languages: How to Express Heartfelt Commitment to Your Mate.* Chicago: Northfield Publications, 1995.

Chen, A. *Ace: What Asexuality Reveals About Desire, Society, and the Meaning of Sex*. Boston, MA: Beacon Press, 2020.

Collins, N. L., and S. J. Read. "Adult Attachment, Working Models, and Relationship Quality in Dating Couples." *Journal of Personality and Social Psychology* 58, no. 4 (1990): 644–663.

Conley, T. D., J. L. Matsick, A. C. Moors, and A. Ziegler, "Investigation of Consensually Nonmonogamous Relationships: Theories, Methods, and New Directions," *Perspectives on Psychological Science* 12, no. 2 (2017): 205–232.

Conley, T. D., A. C. Moors, J. L. Matsick, and A. Ziegler. "The Fewer the Merrier?: Assessing Stigma Surrounding Consensually Nonmonogamous Romantic Relationships." *Analyses of Social Issues and Public Policy* 13, no.1 (2012): 1–30.

Cyr, C., E. M. Euser, M. J. Bakermans-Kranenburg, and M. H. Van Ijzendoorn, "Attachment Security and Disorganization in Mistreating and High-Risk Families: A Series of Meta-analyses," *Development and Psychopathology* 22, no. 1 (2010): 87–108.

Dispenza, J. *Becoming Supernatural: How Common People Are Doing the Uncommon*. Carlsbad, CA: Hay House, Inc., 2017.

Dugna, M. "The Nested Theory of Conflict." *A Leadership Journal: Women in Leadership* 1 (1996): 9–20.

Early, J., and B. Weiss. *Freedom from Your Inner Critic: A Self-Therapy Approach*. Boulder, CO: Sounds True, 2013.

Easton, D., and J. W. Hardy. *The Ethical Slut: A Practical Guide to Polyamory, Open Relationships & Other Adventures*. Greenery Press, 1997.

Fay, D. *Becoming Safely Embodied: A Skills-Based Approach to Working with Trauma and Dissociation*. Somerville, MA: Heart Full Life Publishing, 2007.

Feeney, J. A. "Adult Romantic Attachment: Developments in the Study of Couple Relationships." In *Handbook of Attachment: Theory, Research, and Clinical Applications,* 2nd Edition, edited by J. Cassidy and P. A. Shaver, 456–481. New York: Guilford Press, 2008.

Fey, T. *Bossypants.* New York: Little, Brown, 2011.

Frei, J. R., and P. R. Shaver. "Respect in Close Relationships: Prototype Definition, Self-Report Assessment, and Initial Correlates." *Personal Relationships* 9, no. 2 (2002): 121–139.

Galtung, J. "Violence, Peace, and Peace Research." *Journal of Peace Research* 6, no. 3 (1969): 167–191.

Gottman, J. *The Science of Trust: Emotional Attunement for Couples.* New York: Norton & Co, 2011.

Gottman, J., J. S. Gottman, D. C. Abrams, and R. C. Abrams. *Eight Dates: Essential Conversations for a Lifetime of Love.* New York: Workman Publishing Company, 2018.

Hanson, R. *Hardwiring Happiness: The New Brain Science of Contentment, Calm, and Confidence.* New York: Harmony Books, 2014.

Haupert, M. L., A. N. Gesselman, A. C. Moors, H. E. Fisher, and J. R. Garcia. "Prevalence of Experiences with Consensual Nonmonogamous Relationships: Findings from Two National Samples of Single Americans," *Journal of Sex & Marital Therapy* 43, no. 5 (2017): 424–440.

Hazan, C., and P. Shaver. "Romantic Love Conceptualized as an Attachment Process." *Journal of Personality and Social Psychology* 52, no. 3 (1987): 511–524.

Hazen, N., S. Allen, C. Christopher, T. Umemura, and D. Jacobvitz. "Very Extensive Nonmaternal Care Predicts Mother–Infant Attachment Disorganization: Convergent Evidence from Two Samples," *Development and Psychopathology* 27, no. 3 (2014): 1–13.

Heller, D. P. *The Power of Attachment: How to Create Deep and Lasting Intimate Relationships.* Boulder, CO: Sounds True, 2019.

Heller, D. P., and K. H. Payne. "Secure Attachment Parenting in the Digital Age." 2019. https://attachmentmastery.com/parenting.

Hepper, E. G., and K. B. Carnelley. "Attachment and Romantic Relationships: The Role of Models of Self and Other." In *The Psychology of Love (Vol. 1)*, edited by M. Paludi, 133–154. Santa Barbara, CA: Praeger, 2012.

Hübl, T. The Pocket Project. https://thomashuebl.com/about/pocket-project/.

Johnson, S. *Hold Me Tight: Seven Conversations for a Lifetime of Love.* New York: Little, Brown, 2008.

Johnson, S. Intensive Course in Emotionally Focused Therapy with Sue Johnson: Attachment-Based Interventions for Couples in Crisis. Lesson Two. https://catalog.pesi.com/sales/bh_001234_eftintensive_011518_organic-78213.

Joireman, J., T. L. Needham, and A. L. Cummings. "Relationships Between Dimensions of Attachment and Empathy." *North American Journal of Psychology* 4, no. 3 (2002): 63–80.

Joseph, S. "Growth Following Adversity: Positive Psychological Perspectives on Posttraumatic Stress." *Psihologijske Teme* 18, no. 2 (2009): 335–344.

King, S. "Attachment Security: Polyamory and Monogamy, A Comparison Analysis" (2014). Retrieved from UMI Dissertation Publishing, UMI 3581155.

Levine, E. C., D. Herbenick, and O. Martinez. "Open Relationships, Nonconsensual Nonmonogamy, and Monogamy Among U.S. Adults: Findings from the 2012 National Survey of Sexual Health and Behavior." *Archives of Sexual Behavior* 47, no. 5 (2018): 1439–1450.

Levy, K. N. "Introduction: Attachment Theory and Psychotherapy: Attachment and Psychotherapy." *Journal of Clinical Psychology* 69, no. 11 (2013): 1133–1135.

Life, M. *Spiritual Polyamory*. Lincoln, NE: iUniverse, Inc., 2004.

Main, M., and J. Solomon. "Discovery of a New, Insecure-Disorganized/Disoriented Attachment Pattern." In *Affective Development in Infancy*, edited by M. Yogman and T. B. Brazelton, 95–124. Norwood, NJ: Ablex, 1986.

Mark, K. P., L. M. Vowels, and S. H. Murray. "The Impact of Attachment Style on Sexual Satisfaction and Sexual Desire in a Sexually Diverse Sample." *Journal of Sex and Marital Therapy* 44, no. 5 (2018): 450–458.

Matsick, J. L., T. D. Conley, A. Ziegler, A. C. Moors, and J. D. Rubin. "Love and Sex: Polyamorous Relationships are Perceived More Favourably Than Swinging and Open Relationships." *Psychology & Sexuality* 5, no. 4 (2014): 339–348.

Mikulincer, M., V. Florian, P. A. Cowan, and C. P. Cowan. "Attachment Security in Couple Relationships: A Systemic Model and Its Implications for Family Dynamics." *Family Process* 41, no. 3 (2002): 405–434.

Mikulincer, M., and P. R. Shaver. *Attachment in Adulthood: Structure, Dynamics, and Change*. New York: Guilford Press, 2007.

Mikulincer, M., and P. R. Shaver. *Attachment in Adulthood (Second Edition): Structure, Dynamics and Change*. New York: Guilford Press, 2016.

Mikulincer, M., P. R. Shaver, and K. Slav. "Attachment, Mental Representations of Others, and Gratitude and Forgiveness in Romantic Relationships." In *Dynamics of Romantic Love: Attachment, Caregiving, and Sex*, edited by M. Mikulincer and G. S. Goodman, 190–215. New York: Guilford Press, 2006.

Mogilski, J. K., S. D. Reeve, S. C. A. Nicolas, S. H. Donaldson, V. E. Mitchell, and L. L. M. Welling. "Jealousy, Consent, and Compersion within Monogamous and Consensually Non-monogamous Romantic Relationships." *Archives of Sexual Behavior* 48, no. 2 (2019): 1811–1828, doi:10.1007/s10508–018–1286–4.

Moors, A. C. "Has the American Public's Interest in Information Related to Relationships Beyond 'The Couple' Increased Over Time?" *The Journal of Sex Research* 54, no. 6 (2017): 677–684.

Moors, A. C., T. D. Conley, R. S. Edelstein, and W. J. Chopik. "Attached to Monogamy? Avoidance Predicts Willingness to Engage (But not Actual Engagement) in Consensual Nonmonogamy." *Journal of Social and Personal Relationships* 32, no. 2 (2014): 222–240.

Moors, A. C., J. L. Matsick, and H. A. Schechinger. "Unique and Shared Relationship Benefits of Consensually Nonmonogamous and Monogamous Relationships." *European Psychologist* 22, no. 1 (2017): 55–71.

Moors, A. C., J. Matsick, A. Ziegler, J. Rubin, and T. Conley. "Stigma Toward Individuals Engaged in Consensual Nonmonogamy: Robust and Worthy of Additional Research." *Analyses of Social Issues and Public Policy* 13, no. 1 (2013): 52–69, https://doi.org/10.1111/asap.12020.

Moors, A. C., W. S. Ryan, and W. J. Chopik. "Multiple Loves: The Effects of Attachment with Multiple Concurrent Romantic Partners on Relational Functioning." *Personality and Individual Differences* 147 (2019):102–110

Nordgren, A. "The Short Instructional Manifesto for Relationship Anarchy." log.andie.se. Originally published as *Relationsanarki i 8 punkter*, Interacting Arts, 2006.

Perel, E. *Mating in Captivity*. New York: HarperCollins Publishers, 2006.

Perel, E. Polyamory Experts Speak on Non-Monogamy—
    "Special Arrangements" Discussion Panel. (2014). Video.
    https://www.youtube.com/watch?v=4iDluKrMvYw.

Pieper, M., and R. Bauer. "Polyamory and Mono-Normativity:
    Results of an Empirical Study of Non-Monogamous
    Patterns of Intimacy." Unpublished manuscript. Hamburg,
    Germany: Research Center for Feminist, Gender, and
    Queer Studies, University of Hamburg, 2005.

Power, C. "How Secure Functioning Can Help
    Polyamorous Couples." 2014. https://
    stantatkinblog.wordpress.com/2018/01/15
    /how-secure-functioning-can-help-polyamorous-couples.

Primack, B. A., A. Shensa, J. E. Sidani, E. O. Whaite, L. Y. Lin,
    D. Rosen, J. B. Colditz, A. Radovic, and E. Miller. "Social
    Media Use and Perceived Social Isolation Among Young
    Adults in the U.S." *American Journal of Preventive
    Medicine* 53, no. 1 (2017): 1–8.

Rosenberg, M. B. *Nonviolent Communication: A Language of
    Life*. Encinitas, CA: PuddleDancer Press, 2003.

Rubin, J. D., A. C. Moors, J. L. Matsick, A. Ziegler, and T. D.
    Conley. "On the Margins: Considering Diversity Among
    Consensually Non-Monogamous Relationships." *Journal
    für Psychologie*, 22(1) (2014): 19-37.

Ryan, C., and C. Jethá. *Sex at Dawn: The Prehistoric Origins
    of Modern Sexuality*. New York: Harper, 2010.

Schore, A. N. "The Right Brain is Dominant in Psychotherapy."
    Psychotherapy 51, no. 3 (2014): 388–397.

Schwartz, R. C. *Internal Family Systems Therapy (The Guilford
    Family Therapy Series)*. New York: Guilford Press, 1995.

Selterman, D. F., A. N. Gesselman, and A. C. Moors. "Sexuality
    Through the Lens of Secure Base Attachment Dynamics:
    Individual Differences in Sexploration." PsyArXiv (2019).
    https://doi.org/10.31234/osf.io/zsg3x

Sheff, E. *The Polyamorists Next Door. Inside Multiple Partner Relationships and Families.* Lanham, MD: Rowman and Littlefield, 2014.

Sheff, E. "Polyphobia: Anti-Polyamorous Prejudice and Discrimination." (2017). https://www.psychologytoday .com/us/blog/the-polyamorists-next-door/201707 /polyphobia

Sheff, E., and C. Hammers. "The Privilege of Perversities: Race, Class, and Education Among Polyamorists and Kinksters." *Psychology & Sexuality* 2, no. 3 (2011): 198–223.

Siegel, D. *Mindsight: The New Science of Personal Transformation.* New York: Bantam Books, 2010.

Siegel, D. "The Neurobiology of Attachment" The Treating Trauma Master Series. Main Session #2 (2019): 13.

Simpson, J. A., and J. Belsky. "Attachment Theory within a Modern Evolutionary Framework." In *Handbook of Attachment: Theory, Research, and Clinical Applications: Third Edition,* edited by Jude Cassidy and Phillip R. Shaver. New York: Guilford Press, 2018.

Sinek, S. *Find Your Why: A Practical Guide for Discovering Purpose for You and Your Team.* New York: Portfolio /Penguin, 2011.

Solomon, A. H. *Loving Bravely: 20 Lessons of Self-Discovery to Help You Get the Love You Want.* Oakland, CA: New Harbinger Publications, 2017.

Tafoya, M., and B. Spitzberg. "The Dark Side of Infidelity: Its Nature, Prevalence, and Communicative Functions." In *The Dark Side of Interpersonal Communication*, edited by B. Spitzberg and W. Cupach, 211–252. Routledge, 2009.

Tatkin, S. *We Do: Saying Yes to a Relationship of Depth, True Connection, and Enduring Love.* Boulder, CO: Sounds True, 2019.

Tedeschi, R. G., and L. G. Calhoun. "Posttraumatic Growth: Conceptual Foundations and Empirical Evidence." *Psychological Inquiry* 15, no. 1 (2004): 1–18.

Van der Kolk, B. "Cumulative Effects of Trauma." Collective Trauma Online Summit. 2019. https://thomashuebl.com /event/collective-trauma-online-summit.

Vangelisti, A. L., and M. Gerstenberger. "Communication and Marital Infidelity." In *The state of affairs: Explorations in Infidelity and Commitment*, edited by J. Duncombe, K. Harrison, G. Allen, and D. Marsden. Mahwah, NJ: Lawrence Erlbaum, 2004.

Veaux, F., and E. Rickert. *More Than Two: A Practical Guide to Ethical Polyamory.* Portland, OR: Thorntree Press, 2014.

Wallin, D. J. *Attachment in Psychotherapy.* New York: Guilford Press, 2007.

Woodbury, Z. "Climate Trauma: Towards a New Taxonomy of Traumatology." *Ecopsychology* 11, no. 1 (2019): 1–8.

Wray, B. "How Climate Change Affects Your Mental Health." TED Talk, 2019. Video. https://www.ted.com/talks /britt_wray_how_climate_change_affects_your _mental_health?language=en.

Xu X., A. Aron, L. Brown, G. Cao, T. Feng, and X. Weng. "Reward and Motivation Systems: A Brain Mapping Study of Early-Stage Intense Romantic Love in Chinese Participants." *Human Brain Mapping* 32 (2011): 249–257.

Zeifman, D., and C. Hazan. "Pair Bonds as Attachments: Reevaluating the Evidence." In *Handbook of Attachment: Theory, Research, and Clinical Applications,* edited by J. Cassidy and P. R. Shaver, 436–354. New York: Guilford Press, 2018.

INDEX

*Page numbers in **bold** refer to figures and tables.*